60 Soul-Satisfying Recipes for America's Favorite Dish

Maria Robbins

ILLUSTRATIONS BY DURELL GODFREY

St. Martin's Griffin ❧ *New York*

Library of Congress Cataloging-in-Publication Data

Robbins, Maria.
Chili! : 60 soul satisfying recipes for America's favorite dish / Maria Robbins.
p. cm.
ISBN 0-312-13040-6
1. Chili con carne. 2. Cookery, American. I. Title.
TX749.P64 1995 95-17147
641.8'23—dc20 CIP

First St. Martin's Griffin Edition: October 1995

10 9 8 7 6 5 4 3 2 1

CHILI!

ALSO BY MARIA ROBBINS

Cookbooks

The Dumpling Cookbook
A Cook's Alphabet of Quotations
A Christmas Companion
Blue-Ribbon Pies
Blue-Ribbon Cookies
Cookies for Christmas

Gardening Books

A Gardener's Bouquet of Quotations

Contents

INTRODUCTION vii

A FEW NOTES ABOUT INGREDIENTS ix

RED CHILI 1

- *About Red Chiles* 2
- *Homemade Chili Powder Blend* 5
- *Adding Extra Heat* 5
- *No-Nonsense Bowl of Red* 6
- *Cowboy Chuck Wagon Chili* 8
- *Winter Solstice Chili* 10
- *New Mexican Red Chile Pork* 12
- *Maria's Big Party Chili* 14
- *Lady Bird Johnson's Pedernales River Chili* 17
- *Venison Chili with Black Beans* 18
- *Brent's Chicken Chili for a Party* 20
- *Lamb Chili with Black Beans* 22
- *Chicken Chili in Beer* 24
- *Derby Day Chili* 26
- *Sirloin Chili with Black Beans* 29
- *Southern Seafood Chili* 30
- *Gary's Cincy Chili* 32
- *Midwest Chili Parlor Chili* 34
- *Cincinnati 4-Way Turkey Chili* 36
- *Christmas Picadillo* 38
- *East Coast Chili Con Carne* 40

GREEN CHILI 43

- *About Green Chiles* 44
- *Roasting and Peeling Green Chiles* 45
- *Green Chile Stew* 47
- *Green Chili Con Carne* 48
- *Beef and Pork Green Chili* 50
- *Navajo Green Chili with Lamb* 52
- *Shrimps in Green Chile Sauce* 54
- *Turkey Albondigas in Green Chile Sauce* 56
- *Chicken Chili Verde* 58
- *Green Chiles with Chicken* 60

VEGETARIAN CHILI 61

- *Vegetable Broth* 62
- *Andy Weil's Vegetarian Chili* 64
- *Black Bean Confetti Chili* 66
- *Bean and Corn Chili* 68
- *Vegetarian White Bean Chili* 70
- *Sag Harbor's Vegetarian Chili* 72
- *Tofu in Red Chile Sauce* 74
- *Chile con Tempeh* 76
- *Many Vegetable Vegetarian Chili* 78

CHILI COMPANIONS 81

Beans 83

- *About Beans* 83
- *Some Basic Facts About Cooking Beans* 84
- *Cowboy Beans* 86
- *Chili Beans* 87
- *Stewed Pinto Beans* 88
- *Drunken Pinto Beans* 90
- *Black Beans* 92
- *Refried Beans* 93

Breads 94

- *About Corn Breads and Muffins* 94
- *Basic Skillet Corn Bread* 96
- *Easy Corn Muffins* 97
- *Green Chile Corn Bread* 98
- *Chile Carrot Corn Bread* 100
- *Corn Sticks* 101
- *Piñon Corn Bread* 102
- *Sourdough Biscuits* 104
- *Navajo Fry Bread* 106

Over the Chili 108

- *Toppings for Chili* 108
- *Red Onion Salsa* 110
- *Avocado Salsa* 111
- *Pico de Gallo Salsa* 112
- *Tomatillo Salsa* 113

Hot Green Chile Salsa 114
Black Bean Salsa 115

Under the Chili 116
Under the Chili, or What to Serve the Chili On 116
Basic Buttered Rice 117
Green Rice 118
Green Chile Rice Casserole 119
Brown Rice Pilaf 120
Millet 121
Polenta 122
Roasted Acorn Squash 124

MAIL-ORDER SOURCES 125
BIBLIOGRAPHY 127
INDEX 131

Introduction

. . . if there's such a thing as a national American dish, it isn't apple pie, it's chili con carne.

—CRAIG CLAIBORNE,
quoted in *The Food Lover's Handbook to the Southwest*

Chili," "chili con carne," "bowl of red," or, as Will Rogers called it, the "bowl of blessedness." Call it what you like, chili is not only a dish that every American eats at one time or another, but also one about which nearly every American, with or without justification, considers himself an expert without peer. There are hundreds of variant styles of chili, from fundamentalist to progressive, and the champions of each consider theirs to be gospel and all others to be heresies, if not abominations. Each style, in any case, has its legion of devoted followers, and the divisions that divide the chili world, while all a matter of taste in some sense, also reflect philosophical, regional, and class distinctions as surely as an accent. "Make me a bowl of chili," an acquaintance of mine has said, "and I will tell you who you are."

There are as many colorful and entertaining, if dubious, stories and legends about the origins of chili as there are recipes. Books like *A Bowl of Red,* by Frank X. Tolbert, and *The Great Chili Book,* by Bill Bridges, tell several of the better legends, but as this is a recipe book I'm not going to recapitulate them here, except to say that I choose to believe that chili originated in Texas among cowboys out on the range. Chile peppers, wild marjoram (Mexican oregano), and onions grew wild on the Texas range; beef was on the hoof, and there wasn't much else to work with. Some proto-chili chef cut up some meat, threw it in a pot with water, chiles, oregano, and some wild onions, and came up with chili con carne—a Mexican name for a truly all-American dish. Incidentally, our neighbors in Mexico disdain any connection to the American chili con carne; unless, of course, it is called *carne adobada,* a dish of meat stewed with red chiles.

To that basic chili so many additions and variations have been added that the only constant remaining in each and

A CONFUSION OF WORDS

In this book "chile" will be the peppers, which can be fresh or dried or ground into a powder. Pure chile powder is not to be confused with the premixed commercial blends of "chili" powder that contain, besides ground chiles, ground oregano, garlic powder, ground cumin, salt, starch, and other fillers. "Chili" is the word for the dish itself.

The aroma of good chili should generate a rapture akin to a lover's kiss.

— JOE COOPER, *With or Without Beans*

Later you may heat it up as much as you want, and put the remainder in the refrigerator. It will taste better the second day, still better the third, and absolutely superb the fourth. You can't even begin to imagine the delights in store for you one week later.

—H. ALLEN SMITH, "Nobody Knows More About Chili Than I Do," quoted in the *International Chili Society's Official Chili Cookbook*

every case is the chile peppers—powdered or fresh, red or green.

The meat can be lamb or mutton (often the case in New Mexico), venison (Montana, Wyoming), pork (Arizona), chicken or turkey (East Coast). Chili can be completely beanless; have beans on the side or under it; it can be a combination of meat and beans; or it can be meatless altogether—as in my recipe for White Bean Chili; or any number of other vegetarian versions although, of course, in that case it is no longer chili con *carne.*

In this book I have collected my favorite chili recipes. They are many and varied, but all have one thing in common: For flavoring and/or heat they call for pure, unadulterated chiles, individually selected herbs, fresh onions, and garlic. In other words, what I ask you to do is to throw out your jars of commercial chili powder and, while you're at it, throw out most of the herbs and spices in your kitchen, unless you happen to have bought fresh ones in the last six months. Must you obey? Does it really make a difference? Yes, you must. Yes, it does. Shopping for the right, the best ingredients (for chilis, I do most of it by mail order) is the single most important factor in every kind of cooking, but it is particularly important with chilis, which are, after all, simply stews. Technique, I promise you, doesn't count here. With the best ingredients, chili of any variety advances beyond the category of casual food (a perfectly respectable category when done right, but one that often means, "I didn't care enough to bother") to the status of full-blown dinner party fare. The only other rule about chili worth remembering is that all chili is better if it's made a day ahead. Have fun.

A Few Notes About Ingredients

avocados: Look for Hass avocados. They are small and bumpy skinned, with a dense, creamy texture and a wonderful nutty flavor. When they are ripe the skin turns blackish purple in color. Avoid the larger, smooth-skinned, bright green Fuerte avocado, which has watery flesh with little flavor.

chile chipotle: This is the dried form of the fresh jalapeño, smoked slowly over a fire made with the leaves and twigs of the jalapeño plant. It is moderately hot and adds a wonderful smokiness to chilis and beans. If you cannot find *chiles chipotles* in a local market, they are available by mail order (see page 125).

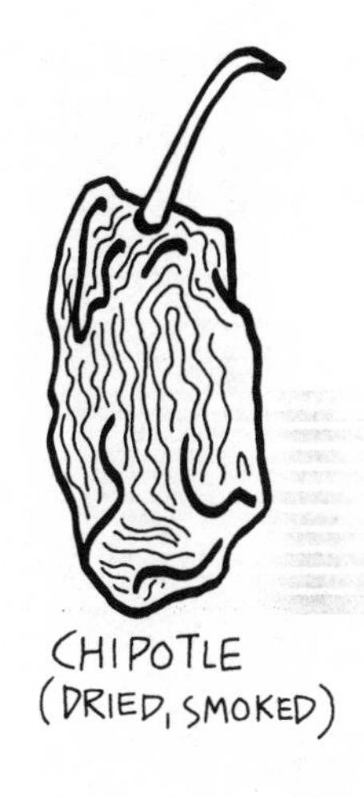

CHIPOTLE
(DRIED, SMOKED)

chiles chipotles in adobo sauce: These are *chiles chipotles* canned in an adobo sauce, which means they have been stewed with tomato, onions, vinegar, and spices.

cilantro: Also known as fresh coriander and sometimes called Chinese parsley. Although it may slightly resemble flat-leaf parsley, the taste is completely different. Strong, pungent, and refreshing say those who love it; unprintable adjectives from those who detest it. There seems to be no middle ground. People either love it or hate it. Use only fresh cilantro; dried cilantro has very little of its original flavor. If you hate this herb, leave it out.

cumin (comino): This plant is indigenous to the Southwest and Mexico. The small brown seeds look a little like caraway seeds. To my mind, toasting the seeds brings out their flavor to great advantage and removes any trace of a raw taste that many people find objectionable. Almost all the recipes call for toasted, ground cumin and the method is as follows:

TOASTED, GROUND CUMIN

1. Place a small heavy skillet over medium heat. Place 4 tablespoons of cumin seeds in the skillet and cook, stirring, for about 3 minutes, until the seeds start to color and emit a delicious, roasted aroma.
2. Remove the seeds to a dish or paper towel and let them cool slightly. Put them in the container of a spice grinder (a clean coffee grinder will do) and grind them to a powder. Store in a small jar with a tight-fitting lid.

epazote: Although it grows wild in parks, along railroad tracks, and in many abandoned places, this is not an herb that is familiar to most Americans. It has a strange, wild flavor and smells a bit like kerosene, but Mexican cooks adore it and use it in cooking all manner of bean dishes to enhance their flavor and to reduce the flatulence factor. To use it fresh, look in your backyard. In its dried form it is available through mail-order sources (see page 125).

olive oil: Olive oil is very flavorful and does not burn easily, making it a great oil for cooking and a good substitute for the lard, tallow, and bacon grease that have been traditionally used for cooking chili and beans. Olive oil adds good flavor without any of the artery-clogging consequences of animal fats.

Of all the vegetable oils, olive oil is the least processed. For the most flavor, look for cold-pressed olive oil that is greenish in color.

oregano: Mexican oregano, a type of wild marjoram, is the oregano of choice in all chili recipes. It has a pungent, wilder flavor than the more restrained Greek oregano commonly found on the supermarket spice shelf. I buy it through mail-order sources (see page 125). In a pinch, you can substitute ordinary oregano in any recipe.

RED
CHILI

About Red Chiles

You can keep your dear old Boston,
Home of bass and cods;
We've opted for New Mexico and chile,
The food of the Gods!
—MILES STANDISH IV, 1842
quoted in *The Whole Chile Pepper Book*

> **A WORD OF CAUTION**
> **When working with chiles—cutting them up, removing seeds, and deveining them—wear rubber gloves. The capsaicin in the chiles can irritate the skin on your hands, rub off on your face, get into your eyes. The hotter the chile, the more careful you have to be. To neutralize the capsaicin on your hands, wash them with a little household bleach.**

There are hundreds of varieties of chile peppers, and you could spend a lifetime studying them and enjoying them. For the recipes in this book I call for a small, "starter" group of chiles, the ones most commonly used in cooking chilis. The one thing I find it necessary to point out is that red and green chiles are not different types of chiles. They are different stages of the same fruit. Chiles are green when they are immature or "unripe," and as they ripen they turn different colors. Some turn red, some turn yellow, and some turn purple. Almost all dried chiles are dried red chiles, although there are some exceptions, which are not called for in this book. Once you get used to the chiles called for in this book in making chili, you can experiment with other chiles till the cows come home.

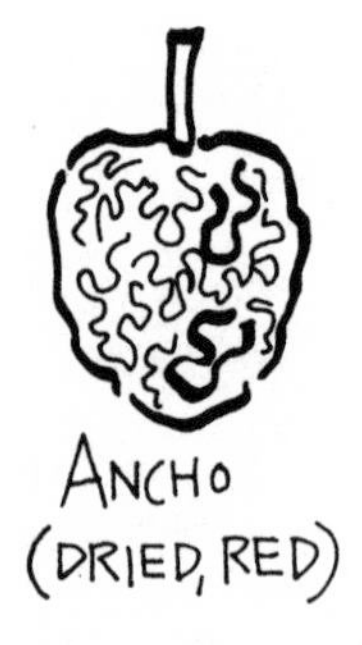

Ancho: Ancho is the dried version of the poblano chile. Ancho means wide, and refers to the broad shoulders of this chile, which tapers down to a point. It is from three to five inches long and brick red to mahogany in color. It is the sweetest of the dried chiles, with a fruity flavor that reminds me of plums and raisins. You can purchase these chiles whole or *molido,* meaning powdered.

Chiltecpins: Wild chiles, the size of juniper berries, grow all the way from the Andes in South America to the southwestern United States. They are called a variety of names: chiltecpins, chilipiquines, piquines, tepins, grains of paradise, and bird peppers. While most small animals, like squirrels, are repelled by the heat of ripe, wild chiles, birds have no problem consuming even the hottest chiles. The seeds of wild chiltecpin chiles were spread from South America to the southwestern United States by fruit-eating birds carrying the seeds in their digestive tracts. These chiles are quite hot, with a heat that passes quickly, and have wonderful flavor that is not overwhelmed by their heat. They are used mostly to add extra heat and flavor to already cooked food. The red pod is crushed between the thumb and forefinger and sprinkled over the chili.

> **Down where these little chilies grow wild, the cowboys eat them as if they were peanuts.**
>
> —FRANK X. TOLBERT, *A Bowl of Red*

New Mexico Red: Unless you live in New Mexico, it is unlikely that you would ever come across this chile in its fresh form. This is the dried, shiny, brick-red chile you will find in ristras all over the Southwest, and it is the chile most often used, in its powdered form, in cooking chili. Often you will find it sorted into heat levels of mild, medium, and hot. You can purchase these chiles whole or *molido,* meaning powdered. Chimayó chile powder is considered the finest of the ground New Mexico chiles. It is grown in the Sangre de Cristo mountains just north of Santa Fe, in and around the beautiful village of Chimayó. The dry, cool weather in this region is considered to produce the best New Mexico chiles.

Pasilla: A five-inch-long, almost black chile with intense smoky flavors. Combined with ancho chile powder and New Mexico chile powder, it imparts a wonderfully complex flavor to any chili. You can purchase these chiles whole or *molido,* meaning powdered.

The heart and soul of any chili are the chiles that go into it. Contrary to popular opinion, chile peppers do much more than add heat to a dish. They provide the dominant flavor in any chili in which they are in ingredient. Unfortunately, chili

When New Mexicans refer to chile they are talking about pungent pods, or sauce made from those pods, not the concoction of spices, meat, and/or beans known as Texas chili con carne. While chile, the pod, is sometimes spelled chili, chilli, or chillie elsewhere, U.S. Senator Pete Domenici of New Mexico made this state's spelling official by entering it into the *Congressional Record.*

The New Mexico State Legislature jumped into the act, too, declaring chile the state vegetable. They got the spelling right, but in their enthusiasm they missed the fact that chile is a fruit. It's actually more closely related to the tomato than to the black pepper, after which it was misnamed. Properly called *capsicums,* chiles range in type from mild bell peppers to the incendiary Habaneros.

—CHERYL ALTERS JAMISON AND BILL JAMISON, *The Rancho de Chimayó Cookbook*

has suffered the same decline in standards as many of our other native dishes, and a chili that is seasoned with commercial chili powder bears a pale resemblance to the original dish.

Commercial chili powders are usually a mixture of an indifferent assortment of ground red chiles, usually already stale by the time they are mixed into the powder, ground spices such as cumin, oregano, garlic, and onion, all of which have a tendency to get rancid, and salt.

If you wish, you can make your own chili powder blend, which will always be superior to any commercial preparation because you control the quality of the chiles that go into making the powder. You can be sure that most commercial blends are not buying expensive, premium-quality chiles, but often use stale, mass-produced ingredients.

Homemade Chili Powder Blend

¼ cup ancho chile powder
¼ cup hot New Mexico chile powder
1 cup mild New Mexico chile powder
½ cup garlic powder
¼ cup toasted, ground cumin
¼ cup ground Mexican oregano

Mix all the ingredients together and store in a tightly sealed container in a cool, dark place.

VARIATIONS:

1. If you have whole dried chiles, toast them briefly (for a minute or two) on a dry, very hot skillet. Remove the stems and seeds and tear the chiles into small pieces. Grind them to a powder in a spice mill or clean coffee mill.
2. I like to prepare the above blend, leaving out the powdered garlic, cumin, and oregano.

Adding Extra Heat

The amounts of chile powder called for in the following recipes should result in chili with a moderate amount of heat to it. Undoubtedly there are people who prefer a hotter chili and this is easily done by supplying chiltecpins, Tabasco sauce, or finely chopped jalapeños along with the other toppings for the chili (page 108).

They put in a handful of chili powder, which in truth is about two-thirds sawdust and one-third red chile.

—STELLA HUGHES, *Bacon & Beans: Ranch-Country Recipes*

PUTTING OUT THE FIRE

If your mouth is burning with the heat of too many chiles, here are five solutions:

1. Drink a pint of buttermilk; this is what professional chile pepper tasters do.
2. Drink milk or eat yogurt.
3. Eat some ice cream.
4. Eat something sweet, like a spoonful of honey.
5. Eat a starchy food such as rice, bread, potatoes, or an apple.

When I was growing up in South Texas, I knew that at almost every meal one of the "kids" would have to run to the back yard for a few Chiltecpins from the doorside bush. Some Texans are so addicted to these fiery morsels that they carry them in elaborate little cases, such as might be used for pills, in order to assure themselves a supply when visiting outside their own territory.
—JEAN ANDREWS, *Peppers*

No-Nonsense Bowl of Red

This is a great meat lover's chili, with a flavor that cannot be compared to any chili using a commercial chili powder. It is quite stark in its simplicity, but I urge you not to fiddle with the ingredients and to avoid the temptation to be creative by adding a little bit of this and that. It might help if you regard this as the mother of all chilis, and one you must taste to use as a standard for all other chilis. If you have never made a chili that relies on pure, unadulterated chiles for flavor, start with this recipe and you will be a convert for life. Chimayó chile powder is the finest there is, and I urge you to keep it as a staple in your spice drawer for special-occasion chilis. But pure New Mexico chile powder is a fine everyday substitute.

2 tablespoons olive oil
3 pounds lean chuck roast, bottom round, or stewing meat, cut into ½-inch cubes or coarsely ground in a food processor
6 large garlic cloves, finely minced or pushed through a garlic press
2 to 4 tablespoons Chimayó chile powder
or
4 tablespoons mild New Mexico chile powder
4 cups boiling water
1 tablespoon toasted, ground cumin
1 tablespoon Mexican oregano, finely crumbled between your fingers
1 tablespoon salt, or 1 large Knorr beef bouillon cube
2 tablespoons masa harina or cornmeal (optional)

1. Heat the olive oil in the bottom of a large heavy pot or Dutch oven until it is hot, but not smoking. Add the beef and sauté over the high heat until the meat loses its pink color.
2. Turn heat to very low, add the garlic, and cook, stirring for about a minute. Add both the chile powders and stir well so the meat is evenly coated. Cook, stirring, for 5 to 10

minutes. Slowly add 1 cup of the boiling water, stirring constantly.

3. Add the remaining 3 cups of boiling water, the cumin, oregano, and salt or bouillon cube. Simmer, partially covered, for 2½ to 3 hours, until the meat is very tender. Stir the chili from time to time and add additional water if necessary. About 30 minutes before the chili is done, stir in the masa harina or cornmeal, if you want to thicken the chili. The consistency of the final chili is up to you. I like mine on the slightly soupy side; my husband likes it very thick. Either way, it's delicious, and like all chilies will taste even better the following day. Simmer for another 30 minutes, taste for seasoning, and add salt if desired.
4. Serve with rice and stewed pinto beans on the side. I like the Brown Rice Pilaf (page 120) and Drunken Pinto Beans (page 90).

YIELD: *6 servings*

CUTTING THE MEAT: Your food processor provides a quick and easy way to get the kind of coarsely ground meat that is perfect for certain types of chili. Using the metal blade, process the meat, ½ pound at a time, for just a few seconds. Any longer than that will turn the meat into a paste. You should have small pieces of meat, not necessarily all the same size. This variation in size gives the chili an interesting texture. For an even more interesting texture, cut half the meat into ½-inch cubes and process the remaining meat to a coarse grind.

VARIATION: You can use whole dried chiles instead of the chile powder for an even richer chile flavor.

Rinse 6 ancho chiles and 4 dried red New Mexico chiles. Remove the stems and seeds. Simmer the chiles in 4 cups of water for 30 minutes. Drain the chiles but reserve the cooking water. Place the chiles with 1 cup of the soaking water in a blender or food processor and process to a smooth paste. Add the chile paste and 3 cups of water to the browned meat. Proceed with above recipe.

> **The original Texas-style chili didn't contain any vegetables except chili peppers, the burning capsicums, a few other spices derived from the plant kingdom—no tomatoes or chopped onions as in the Pedernales River recipe. The original was simply bite-size or coarsely ground beef . . . cooked slowly and for a long time in boon companionship with the pulp of chili peppers, crushed powder from the curly leaves of oregano, ground cumin seeds, and chopped garlic cloves.**
>
> —FRANK TOLBERT, *A Bowl of Red*

> **The daily strategy of a typical spring round-up focused on a moving chuck wagon from which the men fanned out in the morning and to which they circled back with the cattle for sorting and branding each afternoon.**
> —*Trail Boss's Cowboy Cookbook*

Cowboy Chuck Wagon Chili

In *The International Chili Society's Official Chili Cookbook,* Martina and William Neely write about one of the most enduring, romantic notions about the origins of chili: "There is little doubt that cattle drovers and trail hands did more to popularize the dish throughout the Southwest than anybody else, and there is a tale that we heard one frosty night in a Texican bar in Marfa, Texas, about a range cook who made chili all along the great cattle trails of Texas. He collected wild oregano, chile peppers, wild garlic, and onions and mixed it all with the fresh-killed beef or buffalo—or jackrabbit, or armadillo, rattlesnake, or whatever he had at hand—and the cowhands ate it like ambrosia. And to make sure he had an ample supply of native spices wherever he went, he planted gardens along the paths of the cattle drives—mostly in patches of mesquite—to protect them from the hooves of the marauding cattle. The next time the drive went by there, he found his garden and harvested the crop, hanging the peppers and onions and oregano to dry on the side of the chuck wagon. The cook blazed a trail across Texas with tiny, spicy gardens." So why not play a grown-up game of cowboys on some warm, dry summer evening. Cook up some chuck wagon chili and bake up some sourdough biscuits if you're ambitious. Pile your food on the plate, take it outdoors, squat down on the ground in a cross-legged position, carefully balancing your food, and dig in.

- 2 tablespoons olive oil
- 3 pounds lean chuck roast, trimmed of fat, cut into small cubes or coarsely ground in a food processor
- 2 large onions, coarsely chopped
- 6 garlic cloves, finely minced
- 2 tablespoons ancho chile powder
- 2 tablespoons mild New Mexico chile powder
- 3 tablespoons Mexican oregano
- 1½ quarts water
- 1 large Knorr beef bouillon cube

¼ cup masa harina or cornmeal
Small bowl of chiltecpin pods for extra heat

1. Heat the olive oil in the bottom of a large heavy pot until it is hot but not smoking. Sauté the meat over high heat until it is evenly browned. Lower the heat to medium and add the onions, garlic, chile powders, and oregano. Cook, stirring, until the vegetables have softened, 5 to 10 minutes.
2. Add the water and bouillon cube. Bring to a boil, reduce heat, and simmer, uncovered, for 2 or more hours, until the meat is tender.
3. Mix the masa harina or cornmeal with ½ cup water. Add gradually to the chili, stirring constantly to prevent lumping. Simmer the chili over low heat for another 20 to 30 minutes, until it has thickened to the desired consistency. Taste for seasoning and add salt and crushed pods if desired.
4. Serve with Stewed Pinto Beans (page 88), chopped raw onions, and chiltecpin pods on the side. If you want to be really authentic, make up a batch of Sourdough Biscuits (page 104) to serve along with the chili.

YIELD: *6 servings*

VARIATIONS: Feel free to substitute any game, such as venison, elk, or buffalo, for the beef in this recipe. The final flavor will be all the more authentic.

After selecting a suitable spot on the prairie upon which to eat, he executed a marvelous, expert scissoring-down into a genuine Turkish squat, with both hands full, yet never spilling a drop from either cup or plate. Balancing his meal with his hands, he crossed his feet while still standing, then let his knees move outward so that the calves of his legs could bear the burden of his weight as he gradually sank to the ground. This lowering of the body looks simple, but is a difficult stunt if one has never practiced it.

The calves of the cowboy's folded legs then formed the table for his plate. . . .

—RAMON F. ADAMS, *Come an' Get It: The Story of the Old Cowboy Cook*

Chili pangs strike a man when the skies get gray and the wind turns cold. And a bowl of Texas Red is the only cure.

—Trail Boss's Cowboy Cookbook

Winter Solstice Chili

The first time I served this chili, I named it for the winter solstice, the shortest, darkest day of the year and a good reason to gather friends for a cozy, cheering meal. I added the orange juice on a whim, thinking that a dash of Florida sunshine might not be amiss and it works extremely well, giving the spicy chili a nice fruity undertone. The idea for serving chili in a roasted acorn squash is brilliant and comes from a recipe by the great chef Anne Rosenzweig.

- 1 pound dried red kidney, pinto, black, or Anasazi beans, or a combination of the four
- 1 small onion, peeled and cut in half
- 2 garlic cloves, smashed and peeled
- 1 small chile chipotle in adobo sauce, coarsely chopped
- 2 bay leaves
- 1 sprig epazote, fresh or dry (optional)
- 4 slices bacon, finely diced
- 2 large onions, diced
- 6 large garlic cloves, finely chopped
- ¼ cup ancho chile powder
- 2 tablespoons pasilla chile powder
- 2 tablespoons mild New Mexico chile powder
- 2 tablespoons toasted, ground cumin
- 2 tablespoons ground coriander
- 1½ teaspoons ground cinnamon
- 2 cans (28 ounces each) Italian plum tomatoes with juice, coarsely chopped
- ¾ cup orange juice
- 4 pounds lean ground beef
- Salt to taste
- 1 cup finely chopped cilantro
- 3 limes, quartered into wedges
- 12 roasted acorn squash halves (page 124)
- Pico de Gallo Salsa (page 112)

1. Pick over the beans to remove any foreign objects. Wash the beans and soak them in plenty of cold water for at least 6 hours or overnight, changing the water several times.

2. Drain the beans and add fresh water to cover by at least 2 inches. Add the onion, garlic, chile chipotle, bay leaves, and epazote if using. Cook at a simmer, uncovered, for about 2 hours, until the beans are tender.
3. Fry the bacon in the bottom of a large heavy pot until crisp. Add the onions and garlic and cook, stirring, over medium heat for 5 minutes, until the onions start to wilt. Add the ancho, pasilla, and New Mexico chile powders, cumin, coriander, and cinnamon. Cook, stirring, for another 5 minutes. Add the tomatoes and orange juice and simmer, uncovered, for 30 minutes.
4. Meanwhile, in a large nonstick skillet, sauté the beef until all the pink is cooked away. Drain the beef in a large colander and add it to the simmering vegetables. Simmer, uncovered, over low heat, for 1½ hours. Stir the mixture from time to time.
5. When the beans are cooked, drain them, reserving the cooking liquid, and add the beans to the meat and tomato mixture. Add salt to taste and simmer for 30 minutes, skimming frequently to remove any fat that rises to the top. If the chili seems too dry, add some of the reserved liquid from the beans. If it is too soupy, simmer a little longer, until it is the consistency you like.
6. Stir in the cilantro, taste for seasoning, and adjust it to your liking. Spoon the chili into the roasted acorn squash halves and serve with lime wedges and Pico de Gallo Salsa on the side.

YIELD: *12 servings*

NOTE: You can easily double this recipe for a larger party or to store in your freezer.

Chili is not so much a food as a state of mind. Addictions to it are formed early in life and the victims never recover. On blue days in October I get this passionate yearning for a bowl of chili, and I nearly lose my mind . . .
—MARGARET COUSINS, quoted in *A Bowl of Red*, by Frank X. Tolbert

When speaking of a bowl of red, I refer to chili con carne—honest-to-God chili, and not the dreadful stuff masquerading as chili which is served in nine out of ten cafés. Real chili con carne is a haunting, mystic thing.

—FRANK X. TOLBERT, *A Bowl of Red*

New Mexican Red Chile Pork

The sweetness of pork marries extremely well with the mellow, rich flavor of Chimayó chile powder. Because the ingredients in this chili are so basic, I prefer to splurge and use this somewhat more expensive chile. Don't be fooled by the simplicity of this recipe, for it is truly a case of "less is more," and I think that you will find this chili delicious and very satisfying.

I find that 1 tablespoon of olive oil is enough for the browning because the pork shoulder will render some of its own fat as you sauté it. If you should use a leaner cut, such as the loin, you may want to increase the olive oil by another tablespoon.

- 1 tablespoon olive oil
- 3 pounds boneless pork shoulder, trimmed of fat and cut into ½-inch cubes
- 4 large garlic cloves, pushed through a garlic press or finely chopped
- 2 to 4 tablespoons ground Chimayó chile powder
  or
- 4 tablespoons ground mild red chile powder and 2 tablespoons ground hot red chile powder
- 1 teaspoon dried toasted Mexican oregano
- 4 to 6 cups hot chicken broth
- Salt, to taste

1. Heat the olive oil in a large enameled Dutch oven over medium-high heat until it is hot but not smoking, then sauté the pork cubes until they are evenly browned.
2. Turn the heat to low, add the garlic, and stir well. Add the ground chile powder and stir well to coat the meat as evenly as possible. Crush the oregano between your fingers and add to the meat, and continue stirring over low heat for about a minute.
3. Add the broth, a little at a time, stirring constantly to prevent the chile powder from lumping. Simmer the chili, uncovered, for 1½ to 2 hours (add more broth from time to time to prevent chili from drying out or burning) until the

meat is tender and the sauce has thickened. Taste for seasoning and add salt if desired.

4. Serve the chili spooned over Stewed Pinto Beans (page 88), accompanied by Navajo Fry Bread (page 106) and honey; or serve the chili accompanied by hot tortillas with the Stewed Pinto Beans on the side.

YIELD: *6 servings*

VARIATION: Chili prepared in this manner is often called *Carne Adobada*. Substitute 8 dried red New Mexico chiles for the chile powder. Toast the chiles on a baking sheet in a preheated 250° F oven for about 10 minutes. You should be able to smell the aroma of the chiles toasting, but be careful not to burn them. When the chiles are cool enough to handle, remove the stems and seeds and tear the chiles roughly into small pieces. Cover the chiles with 2 cups of hot chicken broth and let stand for 20 minutes. Purée broth and chiles in a blender until smooth.

Brown the pork cubes as described in the main recipe. Add the garlic and sauté briefly, no more than a minute. Add the puréed chiles, oregano, and 2 more cups of broth. Simmer the chili, uncovered, for 1½ to 2 hours (add more broth from time to time to prevent chili from drying out or burning) until the meat is tender and the sauce has thickened. Taste for seasoning and add salt if desired.

Maria's Big Party Chili

During the broiling heat of the midday sun, the military Plaza is . . . as destitute of people as a green watermelon is of hair.

But it is not so after the shades of night have begun to fall. The visitor who strolls around the ancient Plaza, that has so oft resounded to the clash of arms between Spanish cavaliers and the Indian hordes, will observe campfires. He will see an array of tables and benches, and he will be assailed by the smell of something cooking. At the fire are numerous pots and kettles, around which are dusky female figures, and faces that are suggestive of "the weird sisters" whose culinary proclivities were such a source of annoyance to Macbeth.

These are the *chili con carne* stands, at which this toothsome viand is sold to all who have the money and inclination to patronize them. *(cont.)*

Once a year, in the summer, when my husband has a gallery show of his new photographs, we invite lots of people back to the house after the opening. This chili, evolved over a number of years, has become part of the fun of going to Ken's opening. It satisfies many requirements and I include it here because it is a perfect party dish that frees the host or hostess on the day of the party. It can, and even should, be made one or two days before serving. It is hearty, meaty, and delicious and feeds a large number of people without breaking the bank.

Cooking this amount of chili is a lengthy process because of the sheer quantities involved—but you can do it at your leisure, way ahead of time. The most laborious part of the recipe is cutting the meat into 1-inch chunks. A sharp chef's knife is a must, and the resulting texture and taste are worth the effort.

Make sure you have a large (at least 16-quart) pot or two 8-quart pots to cook the chili in. You will need a third pot to cook the beans (I use a 6-quart Dutch oven for this).

FOR THE BEANS:

- ½ pound (1 cup) each dried red kidney, black, pinto, and Anasazi beans, or 2 pounds any combination of dried beans, soaked in water to cover overnight (see page 84)
- 2 bay leaves
- 1 large onion, roughly chopped
- 1 tablespoon oregano
- 2 chiles chipotle in adobo sauce

FOR THE MEAT:

- 10 pounds beef chuck, cut into 1-inch pieces
- ¼ cup hot New Mexico chile powder
- ¼ cup mild New Mexico chile powder
- 1 tablespoon toasted, ground cumin
- 4 pounds Italian sausage
- 1 cup dry white wine
- ¼ cup olive oil
- 4 large white or yellow onions, coarsely chopped

8 garlic cloves, finely minced or pushed through a press
¼ cup mild New Mexico red chile powder
2 tablespoons ancho chile powder
2 tablespoons pasilla chile powder
2 tablespoons toasted, ground cumin
2 tablespoons Mexican oregano
5 cans (28 ounces each) Italian plum tomatoes, drained and coarsely chopped
4 cups beef broth (can be made from 2 large Knorr beef bouillon cubes dissolved in 4 cups boiling water)
Salt, to taste

1. Drain the beans and place them in a 6-quart Dutch oven. Add fresh water to cover by 2 inches, add bay leaves, onion, oregano, and chipotle chiles. Simmer, uncovered, over low heat for 1½ to 2 hours, until beans are just tender. Add salt to taste. Remove bay leaves and set beans aside.
2. Preheat the oven to 450° F.
3. Spread the beef chunks on a large cookie sheet or roasting pan so meat is in one layer. Mix together the hot red chile powder, mild red chile powder, and ground cumin. Sprinkle it over the meat and rub it in with your hands. Roast in hot oven for 20 to 25 minutes, until meat is just browned. Remove from oven, discard any rendered fat, and set meat aside.
4. While meat is browning, place the sausage in a heavy skillet, just large enough to hold it. Prick the sausage all over with a fork. Pour in the white wine and enough water to almost cover the sausage. Bring to a boil on top of the stove. Reduce to a simmer, cover partially, and cook for 10 minutes. Turn the sausage over and cook for another 10 minutes. Remove sausage from liquid, let cool, slice into ½-inch chunks, and reserve. Degrease the liquid in the skillet (the easiest way to do this is to pour it into a gravy strainer cup to separate the fat) and reserve it.
5. Heat the olive oil in the large pot you will use to make the chili. (If you plan to use two pots, proceed with just one for the time being.) Add the onions and sauté for 10 to 15 min-

(Maria's Big Party Chile cont. on next page)

Chili con carne is a dish, which literally translated means "pepper with meat." . . . There is nothing hotter than these little red _chile_ peppers with which the Mexican seasons everything he eats. . . . The innocent stranger who takes a mouthful of _chili con carne_ never inquires what the other ingredients are. His only thought is how to obtain the services of the fire department to put out the fire in the roof of his mouth. The incandescent glow is almost as heated as the language he uses after his mouth has sufficiently cooled down to enable him to use it for conventional purposes.

—ALEXANDER SWEET, in an 1885 newspaper column describing chili stands in San Antonio, *Alex Sweet's Texas*

For those not familiar with real Texas chili, ground beef and beans are heresy. Blends of secret spices, red chile powder, and long slow cooking make its magic.
—MELISSA T. STOCK, *Chile Pepper* magazine

utes, until they soften. Add the garlic and sauté another 5 minutes. Stir in the three chili powders, cumin, and oregano. Add tomatoes, browned beef chunks, and the defatted liquid from poaching the sausage. Mix everything together, then divide the mixture into two pots if you are using two pots. Add 2 cups beef broth to each pot and enough water to just cover the meat. Bring to a boil and reduce to a gentle simmer. Simmer, uncovered, for 2 hours, until the meat is just tender.

6. Drain the beans but reserve the liquid. Add the beans to the meat (divide in two if using two pots). Add the sausage. Stir and bring to a simmer. Simmer, uncovered, for 1 hour, stirring frequently. If there is not enough liquid, add some of the reserved bean broth and/or water. There should be very little fat on top of the liquid, but you should skim away most of what appears on the surface. Taste for seasoning and add salt if necessary and additional extra hot New Mexican chile powder to taste.
7. To serve the following day, remove from heat, let cool completely, and refrigerate until the day of the party. Remove from refrigerator on the morning of the party. Let come to room temperature and reheat slowly over low heat.
8. Serve with rice, taco chips, grated Monterey Jack cheese, Red Onion Salsa, and lots of corn bread.

YIELD: *50 to 60 servings*

Lady Bird Johnson's Pedernales River Chili

> President Johnson didn't have to return to Texas for his favorite bowl o' red—he always carried a supply of Lady Bird's Pedernales River Chili aboard Air Force One. Such is the devotion to just one of the famous foods that originated in the Lone Star State.
>
> —DAVID DEWITT AND MARY JANE WILAN, *The Food Lover's Handbook to the Southwest*

This recipe for L.B.J.'s favorite chili appears in almost every collection of chili recipes, so who am I to leave it out? It is a variation on the classic bowl of red in that it calls for tomatoes, which most recipes for Texas chili disdain. But L.B.J. was a strong-willed man when it came to getting what he wanted. And strangely, although he raised cattle, he preferred venison, above all other meats, for his chili.

L.B.J.'s preferred accompaniments were saltine crackers and a glass of milk. I prefer boiled pinto beans on the side, Pico de Gallo Salsa (page 112) on the top, corn bread, and beer.

- 4 pounds beef or venison, cut into small (¼-inch) cubes or coarsely ground in a food processor
- 1 large onion, coarsely chopped
- 2 garlic cloves, finely minced
- 1 teaspoon Mexican oregano
- 1 teaspoon toasted, ground cumin
- 2 to 4 tablespoons ground mild red chile powder
- 1 can (28 ounces) tomatoes, drained and coarsely chopped
- 2 cups hot water
- Salt to taste
- Small bowl of chiltecpin pods, for extra heat

1. Place a large cast iron skillet over high heat. Add the beef or venison, onion, and garlic to the hot skillet and cook, stirring, until the meat is lightly browned.
2. Transfer the meat and onions to a large pot. Stir in the oregano, cumin, chile powder, tomatoes, hot water, and salt. Bring to a boil, reduce heat to low, and simmer, uncovered, for about 1 hour, until the meat is tender.
3. Skim off any visible fat, or let cool and refrigerate for several hours until the fat has congealed on top. Remove the fat and reheat the chili.

YIELD: *8 to 10 servings*

> **Of all meats, some say, venison makes the best chili.**
>
> —BILL BRIDGES, *The Great Chili Book*

Venison Chili with Black Beans

Venison, with its robust flavor, is a perfect red meat for a hearty chili con carne. It is significantly lower in fat and cholesterol than beef and is raised without harmful chemicals and hormones. Ask your butcher to order it for you or see page 125 for a list of mail-order sources.

This chili is particularly good served in Roasted Acorn Squash halves (page 124).

- 3 tablespoons olive oil
- 2 pounds boneless shoulder or leg of venison, cut into ½-inch cubes
- 1 large onion, finely chopped
- 4 large garlic cloves, minced
- 2 tablespoons ancho chile powder
- 1 chile chipotle in adobo sauce, finely chopped
- 2 tablespoons mild New Mexico chile powder
- 1 tablespoon freshly ground black pepper
- 1 tablespoon toasted, ground cumin
- 2 tablespoons roasted ground Mexican oregano
- 1 tablespoon fresh thyme leaves, or 1 teaspoon dried
- 1 can (28 ounces) whole tomatoes, drained and coarsely chopped
- 2 bottles (12 ounces each) dark Mexican beer
- 2 cups beef broth
- 2 tablespoons red wine vinegar
- Salt, to taste
- 4 cups cooked black beans (page 92) or 2 cans (15 ounces each) black beans, rinsed and drained
- 1 to 3 tablespoons masa harina (optional)

1. Heat the oil in a large enameled Dutch oven over moderately high heat. Add the venison cubes and sauté, stirring frequently, until the meat is evenly browned, about 15 minutes. Reduce heat to medium and stir in the onion and garlic. Sauté, stirring frequently, until the onions have softened, about 10 minutes. Stir in the ancho chile powder,

chipotle chile, New Mexico chile powder, black pepper, cumin, oregano, and thyme. Lower the heat and cook, stirring, for another 10 minutes.

2. Add the tomatoes, beer, beef broth, red wine vinegar, and salt. Simmer, uncovered, over moderately low heat until the venison is tender, about 1½ hours.
3. Stir in the black beans and simmer over very low heat for 30 minutes longer. Taste and adjust for seasoning. Stir in masa harina and simmer 5 to 10 minutes longer, until chili has thickened to your liking. Serve with Red Onion Salsa (page 110).

YIELD: *6 to 8 servings*

VARIATION: If you have strong feelings about keeping your chili and beans separate, thicken the chili with a little more masa harina or cornmeal and serve the beans on the side.

. . . my feeling about chili is this—along in November, when the first norther strikes, and the skies are gray, along about five o'clock in the afternoon, I get to thinking how good chili would taste for supper. It always lives up to expectations. In fact, you don't even mind the cold November winds.

—MRS. LYNDON B. JOHNSON,
quoted in *A Bowl of Red,* by Frank X. Tolbert

Brent's Chicken Chili for a Party

Chili lovers come from every walk of life. Chili attracts truck drivers, celebrities, doctors, lawyers, and schoolteachers. Rich and poor undergo a Jekyll/Hyde–like transformation and mild-mannered pillars of the community show no mercy when the topic of conversation turns to controversial chili.

—JANE BUTEL, *Chili Madness*

Here on the East Coast many people have cut down on the amount of red meat they consume and are looking for ways to replace red meat with chicken or turkey, which if they are skinned are much lower in fat. Chili, a dish that has always evolved with the needs of the day, is a perfect medium for both chicken and turkey.

Brent Newsom, a talented chef, restaurateur, and caterer makes this chicken chili, which is popular all over the summer resort area known as "The Hamptons." It is, in fact, a great party dish, especially for the summer when lighter food is more agreeable.

- ¼ cup olive oil
- 5 large yellow onions, coarsely chopped into 1-inch pieces
- ½ cup finely chopped garlic
- 6 red bell peppers, seeded and coarsely chopped into 1-inch pieces
- 6 yellow bell peppers, seeded and coarsely chopped into 1-inch pieces
- 6 green bell peppers, seeded and coarsely chopped into 1-inch pieces
- 1½ cups chili powder (homemade or a good commercial brand)
- 2 tablespoons crushed red pepper flakes
- ¼ cup salt
- ¼ cup ground cumin
- ½ cup sugar
- 4 cups diced plum tomatoes (fresh or canned)
- 4 cups cooked red kidney beans (homemade or canned)
- 4 pounds boneless, skinless raw chicken breasts, trimmed of all fat, cut into 1½ by ½-inch strips
- 1 to 2 tablespoons Tabasco sauce, to taste

1. Put the olive oil, onions, garlic, and all the peppers in a large heavy pot. Cook over low heat, stirring from time to time, for 15 to 20 minutes, until the vegetables start to wilt in their own liquid.
2. Add chili powder, crushed red pepper flakes, salt, cumin, and sugar. Cook, stirring, for 10 minutes longer.
3. Add tomatoes and kidney beans and bring to a simmer. Add chicken breast strips to the simmering vegetables. Mix well and cook at a simmer for about 20 minutes, until the chicken is cooked through. Taste for seasoning and add Tabasco to taste. Serve hot in bowls with rice, millet, and/or corn bread.

YIELD: *20 servings*

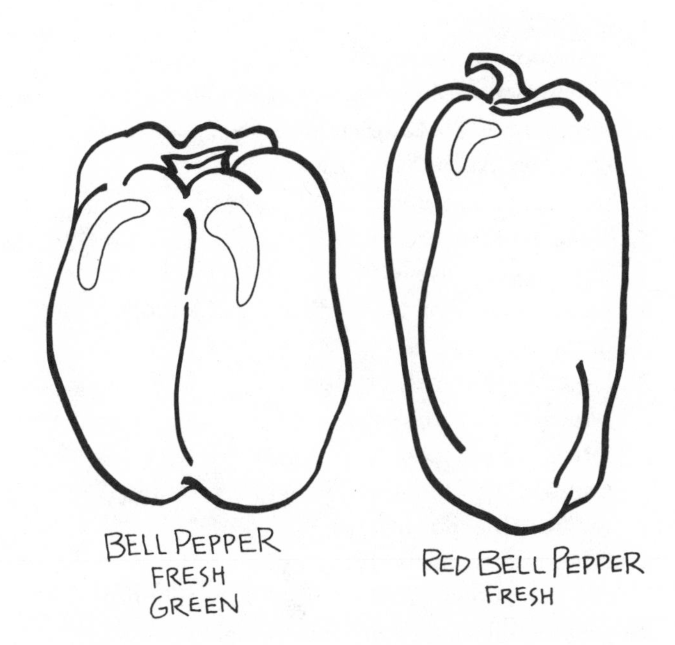

Lamb Chili with Black Beans

Five thousand sheep are on the march up to their summer pasture where the grass stays cool and green. They are heading along an official stock driveway, through cattle-grazing country to higher pasture where only sheep can survive, for a two-month session of nomadic fattening. Ewes and lambs bleat as they walk—mothers trying to find their babies, babies separated from their mothers calling out, and eventually, since each animal has its own special bleat, they locate each other, bounding through the flock and then, always moving, the lambs "mother up" joyfully on the ewes' teats. The flock trudges on, guided by instinct but also shooed forward by shepherds on horseback and little dogs that keep the sheep from straying off into the woods. The herders whistle and hoot and head off the ragged edges of this wooly white mob. The flock flows over the tan road like a huge, low cloud.

—RAYMOND SOKOLOV, *Fading Feast*

It may be that lamb is my favorite meat in chili. Its pronounced, rich flavor seems best suited to stand in partnership with the strong flavors of the chiles. I also enjoy the fact that it is a more natural meat, raised on the land, without any hormones.

This recipe is unusual in that the boned leg of lamb is marinated, then grilled over hot coals rather than browned. This, too, gives this chili lots of extra flavor. A special dish for a festive occasion.

- 3 large garlic cloves
- 2 tablespoons coarse salt
- 1 tablespoon freshly ground black pepper
- 2 tablespoons Chimayó chile powder, or medium-hot New Mexico chile powder
- 1 tablespoon oregano
- 1 teaspoon thyme
- 4 tablespoons olive oil
- 3 pounds boned and butterflied leg of lamb, trimmed of fat
- 2 large onions, finely chopped
- 6 large garlic cloves, finely chopped
- 2 tablespoons ancho chile powder
- 2 tablespoons Chimayó chile powder or mild New Mexico chile powder
- 2 tablespoons pasilla chile powder
- 1 chile chipotle in adobo sauce, finely chopped
- 1 tablespoon toasted, ground cumin
- 1 can (28 ounces) whole tomatoes, drained and roughly chopped
- 3 cups chicken or beef broth
- 4 cups cooked black beans (page 92), drained, or canned black beans, drained and rinsed
- 3 to 4 tablespoons fresh lime juice
- Salt and freshly ground black pepper, to taste

1. With a mortar and pestle, pound the garlic into the salt to make a paste. Add the black pepper, chile powder, oregano, thyme, and 2 tablespoons of olive oil and mix together. Rub the lamb all over with this mixture, cover with plastic wrap, and refrigerate for several hours or overnight.
2. Prepare a charcoal fire or gas grill, or preheat the broiler.
3. Grill the lamb 3 to 4 minutes on each side, just long enough to sear it. The lamb should not be cooked through as it will be cooked in the chili. Remove the lamb to a cutting board and let cool. When cool enough to handle, cut the meat into ½-inch pices and set aside.
4. Heat the remaining 2 tablespoons olive oil in a large heavy pot over medium heat. Add the onions and garlic and sauté for 3 to 4 minutes, until the onions are just softened. Add the chile powders and chile chipotle and cook, stirring, for 10 minutes. Add the cumin, tomatoes, chicken or beef broth, and lamb. Bring to a simmer over medium heat, reduce to low, and let simmer uncovered for 45 minutes to 1 hour, until lamb is tender.
5. Add the beans, and a little water if the chili seems too dry. Simmer for 15 to 20 minutes longer, until the beans are melting into the sauce. Skim the surface to remove any grease. Add lime juice, salt, and freshly ground black pepper to taste and serve hot in bowls accompanied by one of the salsas (pages 110–115), Basic Rice, and corn bread.

YIELD: *12 servings*

> Next to jazz music, there is nothing that lifts the spirit and strengthens the soul more than a good bowl of chili.
>
> —HARRY JAMES, horn player, quoted in *A Bowl of Red,* by Frank X. Tolbert

Chicken Chili in Beer

This recipe was created by Gordon Moore and Shelley Berger, a team of molecular biologists who seem to have a good grasp of kitchen chemistry as well. For years, our mutual friend Michael touted it to me as one of the best chilis he had ever tasted, so I cajoled and pestered until he pried it loose from his friends and dictated it to me over the phone. It is, in fact, a very good chili as well as being quite low in fat.

- 6 boneless, skinless chicken breasts
- 2 tablespoons olive oil
- 4 large onions, finely chopped
- 12 large garlic cloves (or more to taste), finely chopped
- ½ cup chili powder (homemade or a good commercial brand)
- 4 tablespoons toasted, ground cumin
- 2 tablespoons Mexican oregano
- 3½ cups (29-ounce can) tomato sauce
- 4 bottles (12 ounces each) premium beer
- 6 large Knorr chicken bouillon cubes
- 4 cups cooked red kidney beans, or 2 cans (16 ounces each) red kidney beans, drained and rinsed

FOR THE GARNISH:

Finely chopped red onion
Grated Monterey Jack or cheddar cheese
Finely chopped cilantro

1. Preheat the oven to 350° F.
2. Arrange the chicken breasts in one layer in an ovenproof casserole or baking pan and add water to the depth of ½ inch. Cover with foil and poach in the oven until chicken breasts are springy to the touch, about 20 minutes. Remove from oven, uncover, and let the chicken breasts cool in the poaching liquid.
3. While the chicken breasts are poaching, heat the olive oil in the bottom of a large pot or Dutch oven. Add the onions and garlic and sauté over high heat until the onions have softened, 3 to 4 minutes. Add the chili powder, cumin, and oregano. Cook, stirring, for about 2 minutes.

4. Add the tomato sauce, beer, and bouillon cubes. Bring to a boil, stir to dissolve the bouillon cubes, and reduce heat to a simmer. Simmer, uncovered, over low heat for 1 hour.
5. In the meantime, remove the cooled chicken breasts from the liquid and cut into bite-size pieces. Add the chicken and beans to the contents of the pot. Stir well and simmer for another 15 minutes. If the chili looks as if it needs more liquid, add some of the reserved chicken poaching liquid.
6. Taste and adjust the seasoning. Serve with rice and pass the chopped onions, grated cheese, and chopped cilantro.

YIELD: *8 servings*

Derby Day Chili

I love to observe traditions even if they are not mine. One of my favorites is the day of the Kentucky Derby, which falls on the first Saturday in May. My friend Genie Chipps always has a Derby Day party at her house. She bakes up batches of ham biscuits and prepares pitchers of mint juleps and I bring over my Derby Day chili, which started out being called "my meat-and-wheat-and-vegetable chili." It is perfect for early May when the weather can be beautiful but still cool enough for a hot bowl of chili.

A hot chile is a macho chile. From the earliest times chile peppers have been associated with masculinity. In Mexico, the origin and site of the chile's most elaborate development, folklore is saturated with puns and word-plays that refer to the relationship between peppers and the male sexual organ. Size, shape, and color all seem to be implicated in this popular association, but hotness or pungency seems to be the most critical factor. While one variety is actually called the Penis or Peter Pepper because of its characteristic shape, any chile with its seeds removed is referred to by the Mexicans as emasculated or "caponized." The reason for this is clear, as capsaicin, the chemical responsible for the hotness, is frequently present in the seeds of the pepper; once they are removed, the chile loses its "macho" qualities.

—ELISABETH ROZIN, *Blue Corn and Chocolate*

- 2 pounds pinto beans (or a mixture of your favorite beans), soaked in water to cover overnight (page 84)
- 2 bay leaves
- 2 dried chiles chipotle
- 1 large onion, coarsely chopped
- 3 garlic cloves, crushed or pushed through a garlic press
- 1 teaspoon dried thyme
- 1 teaspoon dried Mexican oregano
- 1 tablespoon dark brown sugar or molasses
- 1 tablespoon olive oil
- 1 tablespoon salt, or more to taste
- 1 cup wheat berries, soaked in water to cover overnight
- 2 tablespoons olive oil
- 3 large onions, finely chopped
- 6 large garlic cloves, finely chopped
- 4 carrots, coarsely chopped
- 4 celery ribs, coarsely chopped
- 2 pounds lean chuck roast or bottom round, cut into small (¼-inch) cubes or coarsely ground in a food processor
- 1 pound lean ground round
- 4 to 6 tablespoons chili powder (homemade or a good commercial brand)
- 1 tablespoon toasted, ground cumin

1 tablespoon ground coriander
½ teaspoon ground cloves
1 can (28 ounces) tomatoes, coarsely chopped
2 cans (4 ounces each) chopped mild green chiles
6 cups water
2 Knorr beef bouillon cubes
2 tablespoons brown sugar
1 package (10 ounces) frozen corn kernels, thawed
1 cup whole grain or coarse bulgur

1. Drain the beans, put them in a large pot, and add enough water to cover by 2 to 3 inches. Bring to a boil and reduce heat to a low simmer. Add the bay leaves, chiles, onion, garlic, thyme, oregano, brown sugar or molasses, and 1 tablespoon olive oil. Simmer the beans, uncovered, for 2½ to 3 hours, or until the beans are very tender. Watch them carefully and add more water as needed. Add the salt for the final 30 minutes of cooking.
2. While the beans are cooking, put the wheat berries and their soaking water in a small saucepan and bring to a boil over medium heat. Cook the wheat berries for 1 hour, adding more water as necessary. Remove from the heat and reserve.
3. Heat the 2 tablespoons olive oil in the bottom of a large heavy pot. Add the onions and garlic and cook, stirring, over medium heat for 3 to 4 minutes, until the onions have wilted. Add the carrots and celery and cook, stirring, for 2 minutes. Add the meat, raise heat to high, and cook, stirring, until the meat has lost its pink color. Add the chili powder, cumin, coriander, and cloves. Cook, stirring, for 2 minutes.
4. Add the tomatoes, canned green chiles, water, bouillon cubes, and brown sugar. Stir, bring to a boil, lower the heat to a simmer, and cook, uncovered, for 1½ hours. Stir the chili occasionally and skim away any fat that rises to the top.
5. Add the reserved wheat berries and their liquid, the corn kernels, and bulgur to the chili. Cook over medium-low heat for 30 minutes. Drain the beans, reserving their liquid,

(Derby Day Chili cont. on next page)

The beauty of chili to me is that it's really a state of mind. It's what you want when you make it. You can put anything in there you want, make it hot or mild, any blend of spices you feel like at the time. You make it up to suit your mood.

—CARROLL SHELBY, quoted in *The International Chili Society's Official Chili Cookbook*

and add the beans to the chili. Mix well and add as much of the reserved bean cooking liquid as you think is necessary. Heat through and serve in bowls, accompanied by Avocado Salsa (page 111), Pico de Gallo Salsa (page 112), and corn bread (pages 96–102).

YIELD: *20 servings*

VARIATION: Add ½ cup good Kentucky bourbon with the water and bouillon cubes in step 4.

Sirloin Chili with Black Beans

The Fog City Diner in San Francisco makes a delicious chili from sirloin and black beans, with nary a tomato in sight. This recipe is my interpretation of that suave dark chili.

2 tablespoons olive oil
2 pounds boneless sirloin, cut into ½-inch cubes
¼ cup masa harina or cornmeal
2 large onions, coarsely chopped
6 garlic cloves, finely minced
4 fresh jalapeño chiles, veins and seeds removed, finely chopped
2 tablespoons ancho chile powder
2 tablespoons mild New Mexico chile powder
1 teaspoon toasted, ground cumin
1 teaspoon Mexican oregano
2 large Knorr beef bouillon cubes in 4 cups boiling water
4 cups cooked black beans (page 92) or 2 cans (15 ounces each), rinsed and drained
Red Onion Salsa (page 110)
Grated cheddar or Monterey Jack cheese

1. In a large heavy pot, heat the oil over medium-high heat until it is hot but not smoking. Add the sirloin cubes and brown on all sides. Lower the heat to medium-low, add the masa harina or cornmeal, onion, garlic, and jalapeño chiles and cook for about 5 minutes, until the onion has softened. Add the chile powders, cumin, and oregano and cook, stirring, for 3 minutes.
2. Add the bouillon broth, bring to a boil, reduce heat to low, and simmer, uncovered, stirring the chili from time to time, for about 30 minutes, or until the meat is tender. Stir in the black beans and cook over low heat for another 15 to 20 minutes. Serve the chili accompanied by the Red Onion Salsa and grated cheese.

YIELD: *10 servings*

Perhaps the most famous—or infamous—Texas dish is chili, that fiery "bowl of red" about whose origins there are several theories. I ate my first bowl of chili at my uncle's. I was so young I hardly remember it, but I do recall it was burning hot. My uncle would invite all his relatives over once a month for a big chili cookout. Chili was his specialty, just as my dad's was barbecue and tacos, and another uncle's was fried catfish. I gradually got used to eating my uncle's chili, and another vivid childhood memory is the wonderful aroma of onions and garlic that arose as the stew would slowly cook. I remember it would simmer as we played outside, all of us sensing that it was something that couldn't be hurried no matter how hungry we were.

—STEPHEN PYLES, *The New Texas Cuisine*

Under one striped awning, a grizzled pair of chiliheads, leather-tan and beefy, Marlboro Men gone a bit over the hill, hunched over a cauldron of red, one stirring and the other sprinkling ingredients.

Both had their eyes closed.

I naturally inquired about this. "How come," I said, "you got your eyes closed?" I speak fluent southern, you see. One of the chefs looked fast at nothing, then leaned over conspiratorially. I could smell chili. I could smell Lone Star. I could smell The Truth.

"This recipe is so secret," the old boy confided, "this is so secret, we keep our eyes shut so we don't find out ourselves what's in it."

—WAYNE KING,
in *Food & Wine* magazine

Southern Seafood Chili

For a long time I resisted the notion of a seafood chili. Intuitively it just seemed plain wrong. Then I went to a dinner party where my friend Paul Bresnick, an excellent cook, prepared seafood chili. I was won over. It was absolutely delicious and definitely belongs in any collection of great seafood stews, like bouillabaisse or gumbo. Think of cowboys gone to sea. . . .

- 2 pounds sweet Italian sausage
- 1 cup dry white wine
- 2 tablespoons olive oil
- 2 large onions, finely chopped
- 6 garlic cloves, finely chopped
- 1 large red bell pepper, seeded and coarsely chopped
- 1 large green bell pepper, seeded and coarsely chopped
- 2 celery ribs, finely chopped
- 4 tablespoons Chimayó chile powder or New Mexico chile powder
- 1 teaspoon toasted, ground cumin
- 1 teaspoon Mexican oregano
- ½ teaspoon ground coriander
- 1 can (28 ounces) tomatoes, coarsely chopped
- 2 cups fish broth or clam juice
- 1½ pounds shrimp, shelled and deveined
- 1 pound monkfish or any other firm-fleshed whitefish, cut into ½-inch cubes
- 1 pint bay scallops or sea scallops, cut in half
- 1 to 2 tablespoons masa harina or cornmeal
- Salt, to taste
- Freshly ground black pepper, to taste
- 1 cup finely chopped cilantro

1. Prick the sausage all over with a fork and put it in a skillet just large enough to hold it. Pour in the white wine and set over medium-high heat. Let it come to a boil, reduce heat to a simmer, cover, and poach for 20 minutes. Remove from heat, remove sausage from the poaching liquid, and

reserve. Pour the liquid into a degreasing cup and set aside, then skim and discard as much fat as possible from the liquid.

2. Heat the olive oil in a large heavy pot over medium-high heat until it is hot but not smoking. Add the onions, garlic, red and green peppers, and celery. Cook, stirring, until the vegetables have wilted, about 10 minutes. Add the chile powder, cumin, oregano, and coriander. Cook, stirring, for 2 minutes. Add the tomatoes and fish broth or clam juice and the reserved poaching liquid, with as much of the fat removed as possible. Bring to a boil, reduce heat to low, and simmer, partially covered, for 1 hour.
3. Stir in the shrimp, cook for 2 minutes, then stir in the fish and scallops and cook for 4 to 5 minutes longer. If the chili needs to be thicker, sprinkle in the masa harina or cornmeal with the fish and scallops. Taste for seasoning and add salt and freshly ground black pepper to taste. Stir in the cilantro and serve in bowls, by itself or over buttered rice.

YIELD: *8 servings*

Gary's Cincy Chili

THE CINCINNATI WAY

In Cincinnati, the chili is served in one of five possible ways:

1-way chili: Doesn't seem to exist, but if it did, I suppose it would be just the chili, nothing else.

2-way chili: Served over spaghetti.

3-way chili: Served over spaghetti, topped with grated cheese, and with soda or oyster crackers on the side.

4-way chili: Served over spaghetti, topped with chopped raw onion and grated cheese, with soda or oyster crackers on the side.

5-way chili: Served over spaghetti over a layer of red kidney beans, topped with chopped raw onion and grated cheese, with crackers on the side.

Anybody who has ever been to Cincinnati knows that one of the many charms of this engaging city is the presence of a multitude of chili parlors, all of them serving a chili unlike any in the rest of the United States. This unusual chili, redolent of cinnamon and allspice instead of cumin and oregano, was invented by a Greek immigrant, Tom Kiradjieff, who opened The Empress Chili Parlor, named for the Empress Burlesque that was right next door. His original recipe was never published, but approximate versions abound.

This recipe was given to me by Gary Rieveschl, a Cincinnati native. He had it scribbled on an ancient, stained notebook page from his friend Mark Baldwin, who credited his grandmother with its origin. The recipe contained an element of mystery, which remains unresolved. It calls, as a final ingredient, for 3 "medium to large dog hockeys." Alas, no one seems to know what these are, but if you know, please write to me and tell me.

- 2 pounds lean ground beef
- 1 can (28 ounces) tomato sauce
- 2 large onions, finely chopped
- 3 large garlic cloves, finely chopped
- ½ teaspoon salt
- 4½ cups water
- 5 bay leaves
- 3 tablespoons paprika
- 3 tablespoons mild New Mexico chile powder
- 3 tablespoons celery salt
- 2 tablespoons cinnamon
- 2 tablespoons ground allspice
- 1 tablespoon ground coriander
- 1 pound spaghetti
- 1 pound grated cheddar cheese
- Soda or oyster crackers

1. Cook the ground beef in a large nonstick skillet over medium heat until all traces of pink disappear. Use a slot-

ted spoon to transfer the browned beef to a large enameled Dutch oven and discard any rendered fat.

2. Add the tomato sauce, onions, garlic, salt, and water. Bring to a boil and reduce heat to a simmer. Add the bay leaves, paprika, chile powder, celery salt, cinnamon, allspice, and coriander.
3. Simmer over low heat, uncovered, for 2 hours. Stir the chili occasionally. Taste and adjust the seasoning. Discard the bay leaves just before serving.
4. Cook the spaghetti in a large pot of boiling salted water until done. Drain. Divide into six portions. Top with chili and grated cheese, and serve with crackers on the side.

YIELD: *6 servings*

Among serious eaters in the Midwest . . . Cincinnati is as well known for its chili parlors—particularly the Empress and Skyline chains—as it is for the French restaurants that have been anointed by the *Mobil Guide.* The chili served is so singular that a chili parlor may describe its product as "authentic Cincinnati chili."

—CALVIN TRILLIN, *American Fried*

Chili Parlor: A fistfight at which cooked beef is served.

—HENRY BEARD AND ROY McKIE, *Cooking: A Dictionary*

Day after day I went to Chili Bill's joint a couple of blocks from the school, sat at a scrubbed wooden counter and for my ten cents got a bowl of steaming chili, six soda crackers, and a glass of milk. That was livin'!

—H. ALLEN SMITH, "Nobody Knows More About Chili Than I Do," from *Holiday* magazine

Midwest Chili Parlor Chili

The Midwest's favorite meal-in-a-bowl, not too spicy, not too hot, but very tasty and satisfying. If you serve it over cooked elbow macaroni, you will be eating the very popular dish known as chili-mac. For years, I ate delicious chili-mac at the home of my friends Pat and Bill Strachan (he from Ely, Minnesota, she from St. Louis, Missouri) and I thought it was an odd, but delicious way to serve chili. Only when my husband and I traveled through the Midwest did I realize that what I had been eating at their house was a distinctive, regional dish.

2 tablespoons olive oil
2 pounds very lean ground beef or sirloin, coarsely ground in the food processor
2 large onions, coarsely chopped
6 garlic cloves, finely minced
1 large green bell pepper, cored, seeded, and coarsely chopped
2 tablespoons (or more) of a good commercial chili powder*
1 can (28 ounces) tomatoes, coarsely chopped, with the juice
1 can (8 ounces) tomato sauce
1 tablespoon oregano
1 teaspoon basil
1 bay leaf
2 cups water
1 tablespoon salt, or to taste
2 cans (15 ounces each) red kidney beans, rinsed and drained
Chopped raw onions, for topping
Grated cheddar cheese, for topping

*Gebhardt's Chili Powder is a typical Midwest chili powder blend.

1. Heat the olive oil in a large heavy pot until it is hot but not smoking. Add the meat and cook, stirring, over high heat until the meat is no longer pink.
2. Add the onions, garlic, and green bell pepper and cook, stirring, over medium heat until the vegetables have wilted, 5 to 10 minutes.
3. Stir in the chili powder, tomatoes, tomato sauce, oregano, basil, bay leaf, water, and salt. Simmer, covered, over low heat for 2 hours.
4. Add the beans, taste for seasoning, and cook, uncovered, over low heat for 20 minutes longer. Skim away any fat that rises to the surface.
5. Serve in bowls with chopped raw onions and grated cheddar cheese.

YIELD: *6 to 8 servings*

Drug Store Chili, albeit a plebeian stew, had a very special evanescence and was always full of beans. Also nobody stopped you from crumbling the saltines into it the way they did at home.

It was served in a large white crockery bowl with a plate of crackers, all you could eat for fifteen cents. I don't know what the drug store cooks put in it but it was habit forming.

—MAGGIE COUSINS, chili authority, quoted in *A Bowl of Red,* by Frank X. Tolbert

> Cincinnati eaters take it for granted that the basic way to serve chili is on spaghetti, just as they take it for granted that the other ways to serve it go up to a five-way (chili, spaghetti, onions, cheese, and beans) and that the people who do the serving are Greeks.
>
> —CALVIN TRILLIN, *American Fried*

Cincinnati 4-Way Turkey Chili

This variation on a Cincinnati-style chili uses low-fat ground turkey instead of beef. Don't be dismayed by the unsweetened chocolate listed in the ingredients. It adds a deep, rich, almost meaty taste to the chili. In Mexico, where chocolate was originally used as a seasoning in an unsweetened form, several mole sauces include chocolate among their ingredients, particularly when they are to be used with turkey.

- 2 tablespoons olive oil
- 2 medium onions, chopped
- 4 garlic cloves, minced
- 2 pounds ground turkey
- 1 quart water
- 1 can (24 ounces) whole tomatoes, coarsely chopped, with their juice
- 2 tablespoons red wine vinegar
- 2 tablespoons Worcestershire sauce
- 5 tablespoons chili powder (homemade or a good commercial brand)
- 1½ teaspoons salt
- 1 teaspoon cinnamon
- 1 teaspoon allspice
- 1 teaspoon cayenne
- 1 teaspoon ground cumin
- ½ ounce unsweetened chocolate, grated
- ½ teaspoon ground cloves
- 1 large bay leaf
- 2 cans (15 ounces each) red kidney beans, rinsed and drained
- 1½ pounds spaghetti
- 1 pound grated cheddar cheese
- 2 large red onions, finely chopped (optional)
- Oyster crackers

1. Heat the olive oil in large enameled Dutch oven over medium heat. Add the onions and garlic and sauté, stirring, until softened, about 7 minutes.
2. Add ground turkey and cook, stirring frequently with a wooden spoon, until turkey has lost its raw look, about 5 minutes.
3. Add the water, tomatoes, red wine vinegar, Worcestershire sauce, chili powder, salt, cinnamon, allspice, cayenne, ground cumin, grated unsweetened chocolate, ground cloves, and bay leaf. Bring to a boil, stir well, and reduce heat to a simmer. Simmer, uncovered, for 2 hours. Add the kidney beans and simmer for another 30 minutes.
4. Cook the spaghetti in a large pot of boiling salted water until done. Drain. Serve the chili over the spaghetti. Top with grated cheese and chopped onions. Serve with oyster crackers on the side.

YIELD: *Serves 8*

Despite what Texans like to say to the contrary, chili-mac, or spaghetti red (as it is sometimes called in the Southwest), has been just as welcome there as in the Midwest. Like beans, spaghetti is a naturally compatible partner to chili. Chili-mac is one of the classic, ever popular American hard times foods which remain popular in good times, too. Ike's in Tulsa, along with countless other chili joints in Texas and the Southwest, have offered spaghetti as an alternative to beans with its chili for decades.

—BILL BRIDGES, *The Great Chili Book*

> Animals, after all, have strong opinions about the culinary value of peppers, too. Birds of all sorts, including magpies and wild turkeys, gobble chiles. Ants, however, avoid powdered chile, perhaps because it diverts them from their work. Bedbugs flee the smoke of burning chiles. (Of course, so do would-be sleepers.) Coyotes so detest chiles that nineteenth-century shepherds scared coyotes off by sprinkling their sheep with chile powder. Sharks are said to find peppers so unpleasant that some seagoing Indians of Central America protect themselves from sharks by trailing ristras in the water.
>
> —SUSAN HAZEN-HAMMOND, *Chile Pepper Fever*

Christmas Picadillo

Okay, okay, so it's not what most people think of when they think of chili, but every time I make this picadillo people come up to me after dinner and tell me how good the chili was (of course, I live on the East Coast). I make this often for Christmas Day when friends come over with their children in the afternoon. The picadillo is served in a large bowl and is accompanied by rich black beans and plain buttered rice. It has a very festive look at the same time that the meal is a very relaxed one with flavors that appeal to children and grown-ups alike. Corn Muffins (page 97) and a large green salad will round out the meal.

- 1½ cups golden raisins
- ½ cup orange juice
- ¼ cup olive oil
- 6 pounds lean ground beef
- 4 large onions, finely chopped
- 18 garlic cloves, finely chopped
- 3 large red bell peppers, cored, seeded, and coarsely chopped
- 3 cans (4 ounces each) chopped mild green chiles
- 1 jar (10 ounces) green olives stuffed with pimientos
- 1 jar (3½ ounces) capers, drained
- 6 cups chopped canned tomatoes (three 28-ounce cans)
- 2 tablespoons brown sugar
- 1 tablespoon salt, or more to taste
- 1 tablespoon freshly ground black pepper, or more to taste
- 1½ teaspoons ground cinnamon
- 1 teaspoon ground cloves
- 1 teaspoon toasted, ground cumin
- ½ teaspoon ground cayenne, or more to taste
- 2 bay leaves
- 1½ cups toasted slivered almonds
- 12 cups cooked black beans (page 92)
- Buttered rice (page 117)

1. Combine raisins and orange juice in a bowl and set aside to plump the fruit.
2. Heat 1 tablespoon of the olive oil in a large heavy pot or Dutch oven over medium-high heat until hot but not smoking. Brown the meat in batches until the meat loses its red color. Remove the meat with a slotted spoon to a large sieve or colander set over a bowl, to drain away the fat. When all the meat is done, set it aside and discard any fat remaining in the pot.
3. Set the pot over medium heat, add the remaining olive oil, onions, garlic, and red bell peppers. Cook, stirring, until the vegetables have wilted, about 10 minutes. Add the canned green chiles, olives, capers, tomatoes, and drained meat. Stir in sugar, salt, black pepper, cinnamon, cloves, cumin, cayenne, and bay leaves. Finally, stir in the plumped raisins and orange juice.
4. Bring the mixture to a boil, stirring frequently. Reduce heat to low, cover the pot, and simmer the picadillo for 30 minutes. Remove the cover and simmer for another 30 to 45 minutes, until the excess liquid has cooked away. The picadillo should not be soupy but it should be moist.
5. Garnish the picadillo with the almonds and serve with black beans and rice on the side

YIELD: *18 to 20 servings*

> Saying that the passion for chili is worldwide no longer suffices. On the second day of the 1975 Apollo-Soyuz linkup, the gnawing hunger for chili, known to its victims as chili pangs, occurred in space. Apollo astronaut Tom Stafford got that familiar feeling. His remark to the Russian cosmonauts, "Hey, wouldn't a hot bowl of chili go great right now?" was recorded for posterity by the memory banks at the Houston Space Flight Center.
>
> —BILL BRIDGES, *The Great Chili Book*

East Coast Chili Con Carne

Ground meat and kidney beans, tomatoes, onions, bell peppers, the whole *megilla,* this is the chili, or some version of it, that you will find all along the eastern seaboard and inland to Vermont and Connecticut. Although this is the kind of chili that serious chiliheads call "spaghetti sauce," it is not to be despised. Served with or without rice, but definitely with some sweet corn muffins, it makes a very delicious meal.

- 3 tablespoons olive oil
- 5 pounds lean ground round
- 3 large onions, coarsely chopped
- 2 large green bell peppers, cored, seeded, and diced
- 6 garlic cloves, finely minced
- 4 to 6 tablespoons chili powder homemade or a good commercial brand
- 1 tablespoon red pepper flakes
- 1 tablespoon toasted, ground cumin
- 1 tablespoon oregano, crumbled between your fingers
- 2 cans (28 ounces each) tomatoes, coarsely chopped with their juices
- 4 cups beef bouillon (can be made from 2 Knorr beef bouillon cubes dissolved in 4 cups boiling water)
- 4 cups cooked red kidney beans (page 84), or 2 cans (15 ounces), drained and rinsed
- Salt, to taste
- Finely chopped red onion, for topping
- Sour cream, for topping
- Grated cheddar cheese

1. Heat 1 tablespoon of the olive oil in a large heavy pot or Dutch oven over medium-high heat until hot but not smoking. Brown the meat in batches until it loses its red color. Remove the meat with a slotted spoon to a large sieve or colander set over a bowl, to drain away the fat. When all the meat is done, set it aside and discard any fat remaining in the pot.

2. Heat the remaining 2 tablespoons olive oil and add the onions, bell peppers, and garlic. Cook, stirring frequently, until the onions have softened, about 10 minutes. Add the chili powder, red pepper flakes, cumin, and oregano and cook, stirring, for 3 minutes.
3. Add the tomatoes, bouillon, and meat and simmer, uncovered, for 1½ to 2 hours. Stir in the beans, add salt to taste, and simmer for 15 minutes longer. Serve with chopped onion, sour cream, and cheese, or with any of the salsas on pages 110–115.

YIELD: *10 to 12 servings*

GREEN-
CHILI

About Green Chiles

Now is the time, green chile, for you to season the broth.
(Ahora es cuando, chile verde, le has de dar sabor al caldo.)
—MEXICAN SAYING

A WORD OF CAUTION: FIND THOSE RUBBER GLOVES
When working with chiles—cutting them up, removing seeds, and deveining them—wear rubber gloves. The capsaicin in the chiles can irritate the skin on your hands, rub off on your face, get into your eyes. The hotter the chile, the more careful you have to be. To neutralize the capsaicin on your hands, wash them with a little household bleach. Because they are fresh, hot green chiles can be even more caustic to your skin than the dried red chiles in the preceding chapter.

The green chiles called for in these recipes are:

Jalapeño: This is probably the best known hot chile in the United States. When unripe, it is smooth and medium to dark green in color. It is moderately hot and has a wonderful flavor. Jalapeños do not need to be peeled and are simply cut up and used to enliven sauces and salsas, and as a topping for a variety of other foods. They are readily available in most supermarkets. The canned or pickled jalapeños are not a good substitute for the fresh.

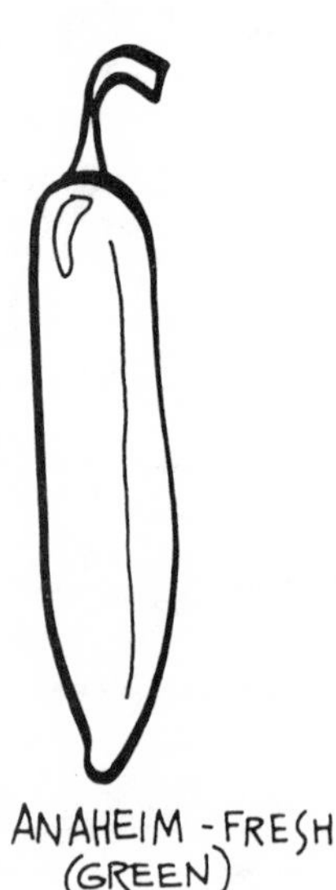

New Mexico Green: Also called Anaheim. This is the chile grown all over New Mexico, and is recognized by Congress as the New Mexico "State Vegetable." It has a wonderful flavor, unlike any other chile—sweet, hot, earthy, and bright—making it the best all-around eating chile that we have. Indeed, in New Mexico, this chile in its red or green form appears at almost every meal.

The New Mexico green chile should be roasted and peeled before eating, and this process further enhances its flavor. The chiles can be frozen very successfully, and if you are unable to find this chile in your area, you can purchase them fresh or frozen by mail order. Roasted and peeled green chiles are also available canned and can be used in any of these recipes. They will never be as good as the fresh or frozen, but they can still produce a delicious green chile chili.

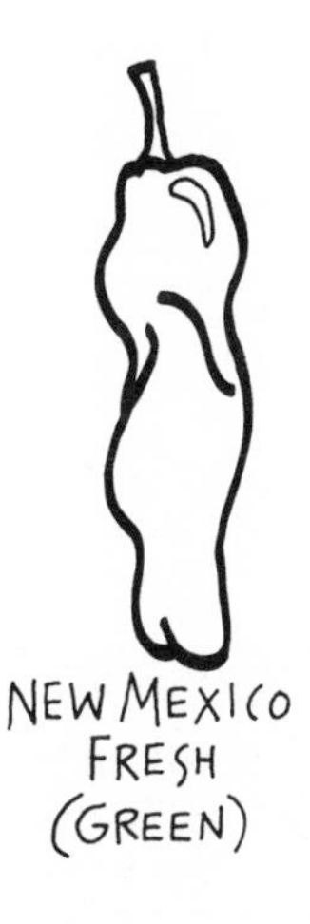

Serrano: These chiles could be mistaken for baby jalapeños. They are the same smooth, dark green color when unripe, but can be only about half the size of jalapeño. They have a clean, sharp, very hot flavor and can be added to or substituted for jalapeños in any recipe, allowing, of course, for their extra heat. They do not need to be roasted and peeled, only seeded and deveined.

Roasting and Peeling Green Chiles

Green chiles need to be roasted and peeled before using them in sauces or on their own. This concentrates the sugars in the flesh, giving the chiles a more intense, slightly smoky flavor. Another reason for roasting the chiles is to be able to remove the skin, which often has an unpleasant bitter flavor. The exceptions are jalapeños and serranos, which are usually finely diced, skin and all.

Chiles can be roasted over a hot charcoal grill, or on a wire rack over an open flame on top of the stove.

1. Cut a small slit in the chile close to the stem to allow steam to escape.
2. Blister the chiles over hot coals or over the open flame on top of your stove. Turn the chiles frequently so they can blister evenly all over. The chiles may burn slightly, but do not let them turn completely black.
3. Wrap the chiles in damp paper towels and place in a plastic bag to let them steam for 15 minutes, or until they have cooled.

4. Split open each chile with a knife and peel away as much of the blistered skin as possible.

The chiles are now ready to use or freeze. Do not keep roasted chiles for longer than a day or two in the refrigerator as they spoil very quickly.

If you know you are planning to freeze the chiles, roast them but do not peel them. Let them cool and freeze them. They will be much easier to peel when they have thawed.

Green Chile Stew

This chili, which marries pork with green chiles, is popular throughout the Southwest, with some regional variations. A slightly more authentic New Mexico version would omit the tomatoes and potatoes, for a very stark but equally delicious stew.

- 2 tablespoons olive oil
- 2 pounds lean pork, cut into 1-inch cubes
- 2 large white onions, finely chopped
- 6 garlic cloves, finely chopped
- 3 cans (4 ounces each) chopped mild green chiles,
  or
- 8 to 10 green New Mexico chiles, roasted, peeled, seeded, and coarsely chopped
- 2 fresh, hot green chiles (jalapeño, serrano, etc.), seeded and thinly sliced
- 1 cup (one 16-ounce can) canned tomatoes, drained and coarsely chopped
- 4 cups beef broth (can be made from 2 large Knorr beef bouillon cubes dissolved in 4 cups boiling water)
- ½ teaspoon Mexican oregano
- 2 large potatoes, peeled and cut into ½-inch dice

1. Heat the oil in a large heavy pot or Dutch oven over medium-high heat until it is hot but not smoking. Brown the pork in batches and remove to a large plate.
2. Add the onion and garlic to the pot and cook, stirring, for about 10 minutes, until the onions have wilted. Add the chiles, tomatoes, and reserved browned pork. Stir in the beef broth and oregano. Simmer, partially covered, over low heat for about 2 hours, until the meat is very tender and falling apart. Add the potatoes for the last 30 minutes of cooking time.
3. Serve in bowls with Navajo Fry Bread (page 106) or with warm flour tortillas.

YIELD: *6 servings*

It was 1952 and I was just into New Mexico from Oklahoma. Something took me to Rio Arriba County. I was up there in Tres Piedras, and I stopped at a little tin diner on the side of the road. The lady brought me a large bowl of green chile stew, and I took a huge spoonful. I've been hooked from that point forward.

—TONY HILLERMAN, in an interview in *Chile Pepper* magazine

Chili mania focuses very simply on a bowl of chili. It is a craving, a passion, an obsession for a simmered combination of meat and chile peppers whose distinctive aroma makes an indelible imprint on the senses. Even the word "chili" is exciting to a chili-lover, for it evokes the memories of a dish that warms the heart and embraces the body in an aura of sensuous satisfaction. Chili is the ambrosia of modern man.

—AL AND MILDRED FISCHER, *Chili Lovers' Cook Book*

Green Chili Con Carne

This type of green chile stew is very popular from New Mexico to California, and versions of it are staples of Pueblo and Navajo cooking. It is very fitting, therefore—not to mention very delicious—to accompany this chili with some freshly made Navajo Fry Bread (page 106) or at least some warmed flour tortillas.

- 2 tablespoons olive oil
- 3 pounds stewing beef, cut into ½-inch cubes
- 1 large onion, finely chopped
- 4 garlic cloves, finely minced
- 2 large ripe tomatoes, finely chopped, or 1 cup canned tomatoes, drained and coarsely chopped
- 1½ cups roasted and peeled mild green chiles, fresh, frozen, or canned, coarsely chopped
- ½ cup roasted and peeled hot green chiles, fresh, frozen or canned, coarsely chopped
- ¼ cup finely chopped cilantro
- 2 cups beef broth
- 1 teaspoon Mexican oregano
- 1 teaspoon toasted, ground cumin
- 2 pounds potatoes, peeled and cut into ½-inch dice

1. Heat the olive oil in a large heavy pot over high heat. Add the beef, onion, and garlic and sauté until the meat is somewhat browned.
2. Add the tomatoes, chiles, cilantro, beef broth, oregano, and cumin. Bring to a boil, reduce heat to low, and simmer, uncovered, for 1½ hours.
3. Add the potatoes and some water, if necessary, and cook for 30 minutes longer, until the potatoes are very tender.
4. Taste and adjust for seasoning. Serve in bowls, with Navajo Fry Bread or warm flour tortillas on the side.

YIELD: *6 to 8 servings*

The California gold rush of 1849 introduced thousands of Americans to chile pepper and chili stew. Vermont-born William Lewis Manly's comments are typical. After nearly dying of hunger in Death Valley in the winter of 1849–1850, he and his friends continued westward until they encountered some Hispanic settlers who fed them a multicourse meal. "Everything is new and strange to us," Manly reported. After an initial round of tortillas (which Manly called "some kind of flapjacks"), their hosts served baked squash and beans seasoned with chiles. "Then came a dish of dried meat pounded fine, mixed with green peppers [chiles] and well fried in beef tallow. This seemed to be the favorite dish of the proprietors, but was a little too hot for our people. They called it *chili cum carne*—meat with pepper—and we soon found this to be one of the best dishes cooked by the Californians."

—SUSAN HAZEN-HAMMOND, *Chile Pepper Fever*

VARIATION:

1. Add 2 cups cooked pinto beans during the last 15 minutes of cooking. Or serve stewed pinto beans on the side.
2. For even better flavor, substitute 8 fresh green New Mexico chiles, roasted, peeled, stems and seeds removed, and coarsely chopped; or 2 cups thawed frozen New Mexico chiles.

> As an army marches on its mess-kitchen, so the cowboy worked with his chuck wagon. The strenuous outdoor work he did required lots of fuel to keep the engine going full steam, and he looked to the cook to furnish this fuel in large quantities three times daily.
>
> —RAMON F. ADAMS, *Come an' Get It: The Story of the Old Cowboy Cook*

Beef and Pork Green Chili

This recipe was inspired by a similar chili my husband and I ate at the historic Taos Inn in Taos, New Mexico. For a festive and delicious accompaniment, make some Navajo Fry Bread (page 106) and serve on the side with warmed honey and butter.

- 1 cup all-purpose flour
- 1 tablespoon salt
- 1 teaspoon freshly ground black pepper
- 1 pound chuck roast, cut into ½-inch cubes
- 1 pound boneless pork loin, cut into ½-inch cubes
- ¼ cup olive oil
- 1 large onion, finely chopped
- 4 garlic cloves, finely minced
- 2 pounds roasted and peeled mild green chiles, fresh, frozen, or canned, coarsely chopped (1½ to 2 cups)
- 2 to 3 fresh jalapeños, seeded and finely chopped
- 1 can (14 ounces) tomatoes, drained and coarsely chopped
- ½ cup finely chopped cilantro
- ¼ cup finely chopped parsley
- 1 tablespoon toasted, ground cumin
- 1 teaspoon Mexican oregano
- 6 cups beef or chicken broth
- Salt and freshly ground pepper, to taste
- Tabasco sauce, to taste

ACCOMPANIMENTS:

- Freshly grated sharp cheddar cheese
- Freshly grated Monterey Jack cheese
- Shredded romaine or iceberg lettuce
- Chopped fresh ripe tomatoes
- Chopped raw onion

1. Mix together the flour, salt, and pepper and spread out on a sheet of waxed paper. Dredge the cubed beef and pork in the seasoned flour.

2. Heat the olive oil in a large Dutch oven over medium-high heat until hot but not smoking. Brown meat in several batches over medium-high heat. As the meat is browned, remove with a slotted spoon and reserve. Discard all but 1 tablespoon of the oil.
3. Add the onion and garlic to the pot and sauté over medium heat, stirring frequently with a wooden spoon, until onions and garlic have softened, about 10 minutes. Return the meat to the pot and add the chiles, tomatoes, coriander, parsley, cumin, oregano, and broth.
4. Simmer the chili, uncovered, stirring from time to time, for about 2 hours, until the meat is very tender and falling apart. Taste for seasoning and add salt, pepper, and Tabasco sauce to taste.
5. Serve accompanied by bowls of freshly grated cheddar and Monterey Jack cheese, shredded romaine or iceberg lettuce, chopped fresh ripe tomatoes, and chopped raw onion to be added as toppings for the chili.

YIELD: *6 servings*

VARIATION: Preheat the oven to 400° F. Scrub 1½ pounds (about 18) small red potatoes. Cut each potato in half, place them in a roasting pan, and rub them with 2 tablespoons olive oil. Sprinkle with salt and pepper and roast the potatoes for 1 hour, or until they are crispy, browned on the outside and completely done on the inside. Use a metal spatula to turn the potatoes over from time to time as they are roasting. Divide the potatoes into 6 servings (6 halves per person) and top with the Beef and Pork Green Chili.

Saturday night chili kept our family together. Mama always made two big pots of chili on Saturday. One was mild-flavored for her and the girls. One was full of mischief, with little red slivers of chili peppers all mixed up with the meat, for Papa and me.

Those pots kept us home on Saturday nights—at least, we weren't about to do any prowling until way after supper was over. And Mama saved enough so we could have chili on the scrambled eggs for breakfast Sunday mornings. I always jumped out of bed early on Sunday mornings.

—WILLIE SCHLIEPAKE, owner of Texas's oldest continuously operated restaurant, quoted in *A Bowl of Red*, by Frank X. Tolbert

> Greedy Columbus, not yet having found the lucrative black pepper he was supposed to bring back from the Indies, hopes to compensate with chilies, so he calls them peppers and starts a worldwide nomenclatural confusion that complicates culinary communication in dozens of languages even today. Of course, chilies did not sweep Europe (except in Hungary); instead, they conquered Asia and Africa and continued to flourish in the warm parts of the Americas.
>
> —RAYMOND SOKOLOV, *Why We Eat What We Eat*

Navajo Green Chili with Lamb

Before the arrival of the Spaniards in 1598, the Native Americans of New Mexico had no domesticated sources of meat, except the occasional dog. By the 1880s there were millions of sheep in New Mexico, and to this day it remains sheepherding country. From the beginning, mutton cooked with chiles has been a favorite among the Navajo and Zuni Indians. This stew, whether made with mutton or lamb, is delicious and authentic New Mexican cuisine.

- 2 tablespoons olive oil
- 1 large onion, coarsely chopped
- 6 garlic cloves, finely minced
- 2 pounds lean boneless lamb, cut into ½-inch chunks
- 2 pounds roasted and peeled mild green chiles, fresh, frozen or canned, coarsely chopped (1½ to 2 cups)
- 2 fresh serrano or jalapeño chiles, seeded and finely chopped
- 1 teaspoon salt
- 1 teaspoon freshly ground black pepper
- 6 dried juniper berries, crushed
- 1 teaspoon Mexican oregano
- 4 medium potatoes, peeled and cut into ½-inch cubes, or 2½ cups canned hominy (posole)
- ½ cup finely chopped cilantro
- Tabasco sauce, to taste

1. Heat the oil in a large heavy pot or Dutch oven over medium heat. Add the onion and sauté, stirring, for about 5 minutes, until softened.
2. Raise the heat, add the garlic and lamb, and brown the lamb, stirring frequently so it does not burn. Lower heat to medium, stir in the chiles, salt, black pepper, juniper berries, and oregano. Add enough water to just cover the lamb and stir. Cook, covered, over low heat for about 2 hours, until the lamb is tender.

3. Add the potatoes or hominy and cook for 30 minutes longer, until the potatoes are very tender. Add more water if necessary.
4. Stir in the cilantro and taste for seasoning, adding salt and Tabasco sauce as necessary.

YIELD: *6 servings*

VARIATION: While it is not at all traditional, I have, on occasion, substituted cooked white beans for both the potatoes and posole. Delicious!

The quarreling that has gone on for generations over New England clam chowder versus Manhattan clam chowder (the Maine legislature once passed a bill outlawing the mixing of tomatoes with clams) is but a minor spat alongside the raging feuds that have arisen out of chili recipes.

—MARTINA AND WILLIAM NEELY, *The International Chili Society's Official Chili Cookbook*

Shrimps in Green Chile Sauce

Does this recipe belong in a book called *Chili!*? Well, if you love the flavor of green chiles as much as I do, then you will also agree that the combination of green chiles and shrimp is a perfect one. But is it really chili? Try it and I think you'll say, "Who cares?"

One of the really great things about this recipe is that once you have peeled the shrimp, the whole dish takes only half an hour to prepare, and yet it makes a superb entrée for a company dinner. Serve it with buttered rice (page 117) and a seasonal vegetable or salad.

- 2 tablespoons olive oil
- 1 tablespoon unsalted butter
- 1 large white onion, finely diced
- 6 garlic cloves, finely minced
- 2 tablespoons all-purpose flour
- 1½ to 2 cups roasted and peeled mild green chiles, fresh, frozen, or canned, coarsely chopped
- 2 fresh, hot green chiles (jalapeños, serranos, or others), stemmed, seeded, and finely chopped
- 2 large ripe tomatoes, finely diced, or 1 cup drained and coarsely chopped canned tomatoes
- 1 teaspoon dried Mexican oregano, crushed between your fingers
- ½ teaspoon toasted, ground cumin
- 2 to 3 cups hot chicken broth or part clam broth
- 2 pounds shrimp, shelled and deveined
- Salt, to taste
- Tabasco sauce, to taste
- ½ cup finely chopped cilantro

1. Heat the oil and butter in a sauté pan over medium-high heat until the butter starts to foam. Lower the heat, add the onion, and cook, stirring, for 5 minutes, until the onion has softened. Add the garlic and cook 3 minutes longer.

2. Sprinkle the flour over the onions and cook, stirring, for 5 minutes longer to make a roux. Add the chiles, tomatoes, oregano, and cumin. Cook, stirring, for 3 minutes.
4. Stir in 2 cups of chicken broth, add the shrimp, stir, and bring the mixture to a boil. Reduce heat and simmer for 15 to 20 minutes, until the shrimp are cooked through. Add more chicken broth to achieve the desired consistency. I like it fairly soupy so that there's lots of sauce. Taste for seasoning, adding salt and Tabasco sauce as necessary. Stir in the cilantro and serve over rice, with Refried Beans (page 93) on the side.

YIELD: *6 servings*

VARIATIONS:
1. For a slightly thicker, somewhat heartier chili, add 2 cups (one 15-ounce can) of cooked white beans along with the shrimp.
2. Any leftovers are delicious over pasta, and I usually make enough to enjoy a second meal this way.
3. Tabasco's new green jalapeño sauce is particularly delicious with this and all the other green chilis.

The turkey was the only domesticated food animal contributed by the New World. Unknown here were the pigs, the chickens, the cows, the sheep, and goats so heavily utilized by the rest of the world. Unknown as well, therefore, were the derivative products of these animals—the eggs, the dairy products, the animal fats.

—ELISABETH ROZIN, *Blue Corn and Chocolate*

Turkey Albondigas in Green Chile Sauce

Albondigas are meatballs. The word comes from Spain, with roots in the Arab language, where, I'm told, it means "to swim." But these tasty meatballs, swimming in green chile-flavored broth, are entirely New World in their flavoring. Whatever the origins, they make really good eating.

FOR THE ALBONDIGAS:

- 4 slices white bread, crusts removed
- ½ cup warm milk
- 2 pounds ground turkey
- 2 eggs, lightly beaten
- 1 small onion, finely chopped
- 2 garlic cloves, finely minced
- 2 teaspoons salt
- ½ teaspoon freshly ground black pepper
- 1 tablespoon olive oil
- 1 tablespoon unsalted butter

FOR THE CHILE SAUCE:

- 1 medium onion, finely chopped
- 1 tablespoon olive oil
- 2 tablespoons all-purpose flour
- 2 tablespoons mild New Mexico chile powder
- 3 garlic cloves, finely minced
- 1 can (14 ounces) tomatoes, drained and coarsely chopped
- 1 can (4 ounces) mild green chiles, drained and finely chopped
- 1 can (4 ounces) hot green chiles, drained and finely chopped
- 4 cups hot beef or chicken broth
- Salt, to taste
- ½ cup finely chopped cilantro

1. Tear the bread into small pieces and soak them in the milk.

2. Place the turkey in a large mixing bowl. Squeeze the milk out of the bread and crumble the bread into the turkey mixture. Add the eggs, onion, garlic, salt, and freshly ground black pepper. Mix everything thoroughly with your hands.
3. Shape the mixture into small balls, about ½ inch in diameter.
4. Heat the olive oil and butter in a large skillet over medium heat until the butter starts to foam. Sauté the albondigas over medium-high heat until browned on all sides. They do not need to be cooked through. Set aside while you prepare the sauce.
5. In a heavy pot or Dutch oven, cook the onion in the olive oil over low heat for about 10 minutes, until the onion is lightly browned. Sprinkle the flour over the onion and cook, stirring, for about 3 minutes. Stir in the chile powder and cook, stirring, for 3 minutes longer. Stir in the garlic, tomatoes, and chiles and cook, stirring, for 1 minute.
6. Stir in the broth, bring to a boil, and reduce heat to low. Add the albondigas, scraping up all the little browned bits from the bottom of the skillet. Cover the pot and simmer over very low heat for 20 to 30 minutes, until the albondigas are cooked through. Taste for seasoning and add salt if it is needed. Stir in the cilantro and serve over rice or little roasted potatoes (page 50).

YIELD: *6 servings*

SUBSTITUTIONS:

1. You can substitute any other ground meat for the turkey: chicken, veal, beef, pork, or lamb. Just follow the same procedure.
2. If you have trouble finding canned hot green chiles, substitute another can of mild green chiles and add 1 fresh green jalapeño, seeded and diced, and 1 fresh green serrano, seeded and diced.

Chicken Chili Verde

One sure sign of autumn approaching in New Mexico is the distinctive smell of roasting green chile. At this time, when the local harvest is at its peak, the Jaramillos serve the roasted chile as a side dish. The roasting process blisters the inedible skin, allowing it to be removed easily, and mellows the pods' pungent flavor.

Throughout Chimayó and the rest of New Mexico, families and neighbors roast chiles by the bushel or 40-pound sack. Fresh-picked chiles fill large wire cages that rotate on a spit over an open fire. Some of the chiles are devoured while still warm, and much of the crop is frozen for the rest of the year.

—CHERYL ALTERS JAMISON AND BILL JAMISON, *The Rancho de Chimayó Cookbook*

You will sometimes find this type of green chili referred to as White Chili, or even Chili Blanco. It is a light-tasting chili, perfectly suited to today's low-fat cooking style. The dark meat of chicken thighs stands up well to the long simmering and adds a rich flavor to the chili.

1 pound Great Northern beans, or any other white bean
2 bay leaves
3 pounds chicken thighs, skin and all visible fat removed
1 small onion, peeled and stuck with 2 cloves
2 garlic cloves, unpeeled
A few celery leaves
4 parsley sprigs
2 tablespoons olive oil
2 medium onions, chopped fine
6 garlic cloves, chopped
1 teaspoon Mexican oregano, crumbled between your fingers
½ teaspoon toasted, ground cumin
1½ cups roasted and peeled mild green chiles, fresh, frozen, or canned, coarsely chopped (three 4-ounce cans)
¼ teaspoon cayenne
4 cups chicken broth
1 tablespoon salt
Tabasco sauce, to taste
Grated Monterey Jack cheese

1. Pick over the beans to remove any foreign objects. Wash the beans and soak them in water for at least 6 hours or overnight, changing the water several times.
2. Drain the beans and put them in a large heavy pot. Add bay leaves and enough cold water to cover by 2 inches. Bring to a boil, reduce heat to low, and simmer uncovered, for 2½ to 3 hours, until beans are tender. Add more water from time to time if necessary. Drain the beans, discard the bay leaves, and return the beans to the pot.
3. In another pot, place the chicken thighs, the onion stuck with cloves, the 2 garlic cloves, celery leaves, and parsley.

Add 6 cups of water or more to just cover the chicken. Bring to a boil, reduce heat to low, and simmer, uncovered, for 1 to 1½ hours, until the chicken is very tender. Remove from the heat and let the chicken cool in the broth.

4. Remove the chicken from the broth. Strain the broth, de-grease it, and set aside. Remove the meat from the bones and discard them. Shred the meat with your fingers into bite-size pieces and reserve.
5. Heat the olive oil in a heavy skillet over medium heat. Add the onions and sauté, stirring, for 5 minutes, until onions have softened. Add the 6 garlic cloves and cook, stirring, for 3 more minutes. Stir in the oregano, cumin, green chiles, and cayenne. Cook for 1 minute longer and add all the ingredients in the skillet to the beans.
6. Add reserved chicken, 4 cups chicken broth, and salt. Stir and simmer over low heat for 30 minutes. Taste and adjust the seasoning, adding salt and Tabasco sauce as needed. Serve hot in bowls and pass the grated Monterey Jack cheese for topping.

YIELD: *6 servings*

VARIATION: For a lighter dish, leave out the beans and serve the chicken in green chile sauce to wrap in warm tortillas.

> **Hotness in chile comes from a chemical compound called capsaicin, found in the seeds and white membranes inside the fruit. Capsaicin is what gives ginger ale and ginger beef that "hot" taste. As little as one part capsaicin to a hundred thousand can be detected by human taste buds. This hotness intensifies as chiles mature.**
>
> —BILL BRIDGES, *The Great Chili Book*

Green Chiles with Chicken

Despite its simplicity, this green chili is utterly delicious, particularly if you serve it with Navajo Fry Bread (page 106), with butter and honey. My friend Becky Okrent, a very talented cook, sent me the recipe, which she has made for years.

2 tablespoons olive oil
2 large onions, coarsely chopped
4 garlic cloves, finely chopped
4 pounds chicken thighs, boned, skinned, and cut into 1-inch chunks
2 cans (4 ounces each) chopped mild green chiles*
2 large ripe tomatoes, coarsely chopped, or 1 cup drained and coarsely chopped canned tomatoes
Salt and freshly ground black pepper, to taste
½ cup finely chopped cilantro

1. Heat the oil in a large casserole or Dutch oven over medium-high heat. Add the onions and garlic and cook, stirring, until the onions wilt, about 10 minutes. Add the chicken and cook, stirring, for another 10 minutes.
2. Add the chiles, tomatoes, salt, and black pepper and about 2 cups of water, just enough to cover the meat. Bring to a boil, reduce heat to low, and simmer for 45 minutes to 1 hour, until the chicken is very tender. Stir in the cilantro and serve.

YIELD: *6 to 8 servings*

*For even better flavor, substitute 8 fresh green New Mexico or Anaheim chiles, when you can find them. Roast and peel them according to the directions on page 45.

VEGETARIAN
CHILI

> Chili's a lot like sex: When it's good it's great, and even when it's bad, it's not so bad.
>
> —BILL BOLDENWECK, quoted in *The New York Public Library Book of 20th Century American Quotations*

Vegetable Broth

I am not a vegetarian, although I enjoy and prepare many vegetarian meals. But I have always had a problem with vegetable broth because I've found it to lack both the depth of flavor and the slightly gelatinous texture that I look for in a good chicken or beef broth. But with a lot of trial and error I have found that by using a lot (sometimes two or three heads) of garlic and adding potato peels, kombu seaweed, and some heat from chiltecpin pods or cayenne, I get a delicious, full-flavored broth.

This vegetable broth will keep for several days in the refrigerator, but should be frozen if you want to keep it around for any longer than that. It will keep in the freezer for several months.

2	tablespoons flavorful olive oil
1	large onion, coarsely chopped
2	celery ribs, some leaves included, coarsely chopped
2	large carrots, coarsely chopped
12 to 18	garlic cloves, unpeeled and smashed
2	leeks, white and pale green parts only, thinly sliced
½	pound sliced mushrooms
2	2-inch pieces of kombu seaweed (optional)
	Peel from 2 large baking potatoes (optional)
½	cup finely chopped parsley, including the stems
¼	cup chopped fresh basil
2	bay leaves
1	teaspoon dried marjoram
3	sprigs fresh thyme, or ½ teaspoon dried
1	teaspoon salt, or to taste
10	whole black peppercorns
1 or 2	chiltecpin pods, or ¼ teaspoon cayenne (optional)

1. Heat the olive oil in a large heavy saucepan over medium heat and sauté the onion, celery, and carrots until they start to color, 10 to 15 minutes.
2. Stir in the garlic, leeks, and mushrooms and cook, stirring, for 5 minutes longer.

3. Add 3 quarts water, the optional kombu seaweed and potato peels, parsley, basil, bay leaves, marjoram, thyme, salt, peppercorns, and optional chiltecpin pods or cayenne. Bring to a boil, reduce heat to low, and simmer, partially covered, for a minimum of 30 minutes and preferably for as long as 2 hours.
4. Strain the stock through a sieve, pressing the solids down with a wooden spoon to extract all the liquid. Taste for seasoning and add salt, pepper, and cayenne to taste.

YIELD: *8 to 10 cups*

VARIATION: All sorts of ingredients from your vegetable bin can make their way into a vegetable stock. Consider turnips, parsnips, zucchini, shredded salad greens, spinach, and fennel. I leave out vegetables with strong flavors such as cabbage, broccoli, beets, bell peppers, asparagus, etc.

> **The near end of the street was rather dark and had mostly vegetable shops. Abundance of vegetables—piles of white and green fennel, like celery, and great sheaves of young, purplish, sea-dust-coloured artichokes, nodding their buds, piles of great radishes, scarlet and bluey purple, carrots, long strings of dried figs, mountains of big oranges, scarlet large peppers, a large slice of pumpkin, a great mass of colours and vegetable freshnesses . . .**
>
> —D.H. LAWRENCE, *Sea and Sardinia*

> **Learning about and understanding dried chiles is very much like developing an appreciation for fine wines—it is largely a matter of educating the palate so that it becomes sensitive to the range and depth of flavors present.**
> —MARK MILLER, *The Great Chile Book*

Andy Weil's Vegetarian Chili

Dr. Andrew Weil is well known for his many achievements in medical research and for his books and articles concerning alternative medicines and treatments. He is perhaps less well known for his talents as a marvelous and innovative vegetarian cook. I have been lucky enough to be a guest at his dinner table a number of times when he was living in my part of the world, and years later those meals remain vivid and inspiring in my memory.

This recipe is my favorite of the vegetarian chili recipes in this book.

- 1 pound (2 cups) Anasazi beans
- 4 tablespoons olive oil
- 2 large onions, sliced into half rounds
- 1 tablespoon mild red New Mexico chile powder
- 3 to 4 chiles chipotle in adobo sauce, finely chopped
- 1 tablespoon Mexican oregano
- 1 tablespoon toasted, ground cumin
- ½ teaspoon ground allspice
- 1 teaspoon salt
- 1 can (28 ounces) crushed tomatoes
- 3 large carrots, scraped and sliced into rounds
- 8 ounces fresh shiitake or porcini mushrooms, thinly sliced (optional)
- 5 large garlic cloves, mashed through a garlic press
- Dash or two of balsamic vinegar, or more to taste
- Tabasco sauce, to taste

GARNISHES:

Chopped raw onion
Grated Monterey Jack or cheddar cheese
Coarsely chopped fresh tomatoes
Shredded romaine lettuce
Finely chopped cilantro
Fresh lime wedges
or
Any of the salsas on pages 110–115

1. Pick over the beans to remove any foreign objects. Wash the beans and soak them in water for at least 4 hours or overnight, changing the water several times.
2. Drain the beans and place them in a large pot with enough water to cover the beans by 2 inches. Bring the beans to a boil, lower the heat, partially cover the pot, and simmer the beans for 2 hours. Stir the beans from time to time and make sure that the level of water remains 2 inches above the surface of the beans.
3. In the meantime, heat 3 tablespoons of the olive oil in a large skillet over medium heat. Add the onions and sauté for about 10 minutes, until they turn golden. Add the chile powder, chipotle chile, oregano, cumin, allspice, and salt. Cook, stirring, for 2 minutes and add the tomatoes. Simmer for 5 minutes, then add this mixture to the beans along with the carrots, mushrooms, and garlic. Simmer, uncovered, over low heat for about 1 hour, until the beans become creamy and start to melt into the liquid.
4. Correct the seasonings, adding more chile if you want a hotter flavor, and balsamic vinegar and Tabasco sauce to taste. Serve in bowls accompanied by your choice of garnishes or toppings.

YIELD: *6 servings*

VARIATION: For the diehard meat eaters among you, grill a strip steak or two, cut into thin slices, and use as topping for the chili.

It is beneficial to one's health not to be carnivorous. The strongest animals, such as the bull, are vegetarians. Look at me. I have ten times as much good health and energy as a meat-eater.
—GEORGE BERNARD SHAW, *The George Bernard Shaw Vegetarian Cookbook*

Black Bean Confetti Chili

This chili is based on a favorite black bean salad, which always enlivens a buffet table with its colorful accents of red and yellow. Translated into a chili it works extremely well. The addition of chocolate may sound strange, but gives this vegetarian chili a rich depth of flavor that will make even the most ardent carnivore forget about meat. The bulgur provides a background texture similar to that of ground beef.

- 2 tablespoons olive oil
- 2 large onions, coarsely chopped
- 6 garlic cloves, finely minced or pushed through a garlic press
- 2 large red bell peppers, cored, seeded, and coarsely chopped
- 1 large yellow bell pepper, cored, seeded, and coarsely chopped
- 1 fresh jalapeño chile, cored and seeded and finely minced
- 2 tablespoons ancho chile powder
- 2 tablespoons mild New Mexico chile powder
- 1 tablespoon toasted, ground cumin
- 4 cups vegetable broth (page 62) or water
- ½ cup bulgur
- 1 ounce (1 square) unsweetened chocolate, grated
- 1 can (28 ounces) tomatoes, drained and coarsely chopped
- 8 cups cooked black beans (page 92) or 4 cans (15 ounces each), rinsed and drained
- 2 cups fresh corn kernels, or 1 package (10 ounces) frozen corn kernels, thawed
- Red Onion Salsa (page 110)

1. Heat the oil in a large heavy pot over medium heat. Add the onions and garlic and cook, stirring, for a few minutes until the onions have wilted. Add the bell peppers, jalapeño, chile powders, and cumin and cook, stirring, for 3 to 5 minutes longer, until the peppers have softened.

2. Add the vegetable broth or water, bulgur, grated chocolate, tomatoes, and beans. Bring to a boil, lower heat, and simmer gently for 25 minutes. Add the corn kernels, stir, and cook 5 minutes longer.
3. Serve with salsa on the side for garnish.

YIELD: *8 to 10 servings*

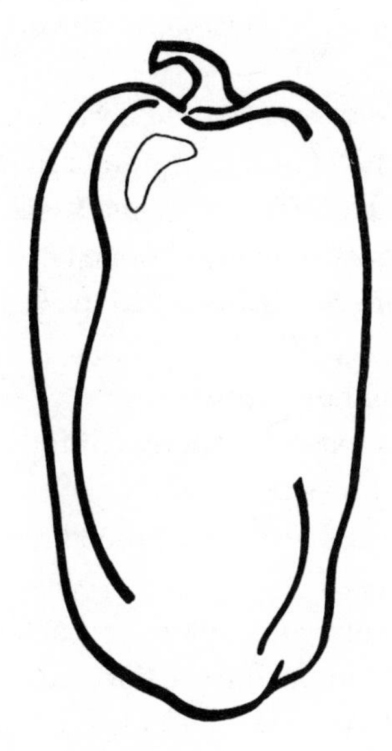

> Vegetarians have wicked, shifty eyes, and laugh in a cold calculating manner. They pinch little children, steal stamps, drink water, favor beards.
>
> —J.B. MORTON, quoted in *The Penguin Dictionary of Modern Humorous Quotations*

NEVER HEARD OF CHICOS?
Chicos, also known as *chicos de horno,* are sweet corn kernels that have been dried without the lime treatment that posole receives. These dried sweet corn kernels have a much more intense corn flavor and chewier texture than fresh corn. It is very popular in the Southwest and among the Pennsylvania Dutch.

Bean and Corn Chili

This recipe calls for dried beans and a particularly delicious dried corn called *chicos.* Although this recipe is completely fat free, it is full of flavor and very satisfying. When served in roasted acorn squash halves and topped with one of the salsas on pages 110–115, it makes a very healthy, colorful dish.

- 1 pound red kidney beans, or any other red or pinkish beans
- 1 cup chicos or sweet dried corn
- 2 dried ancho chiles, stems and seeds removed
- 1 dried pasilla chile, stems and seeds removed
- 2 large onions, coarsely chopped
- 6 large garlic cloves, smashed, peeled, and coarsely chopped
- 1 tablespoon light brown sugar
- 2 teaspoons toasted, ground cumin
- 1 teaspoon Mexican oregano
- 2 cups chopped, drained, canned tomatoes
- 1 to 2 teaspoons salt
- 8 roasted acorn squash halves (page 124)
- ½ cup finely chopped fresh coriander
- Shredded Monterey Jack cheese (optional)
- Sour cream (optional)

1. Pick over the beans to remove any foreign objects. Wash the beans and soak them in water for at least 6 hours or overnight, changing the water several times.
2. Rinse the chicos in several changes of cold water, and soak them overnight in 4 cups of water in a large heavy pot in which you will cook the chili.
3. On the following day, cover the chiles with hot water and let them soak for 10 minutes. Purée the chiles with ½ cup of the soaking water in a blender to a smooth paste.
4. Drain the beans and add them to the chicos in their soaking liquid. Add the puréed chiles, onions, garlic, brown sugar, cumin, and oregano. Add enough water (if necessary) to just cover the beans. Bring to a boil, reduce heat to a simmer, and cook, partially covered, for about 2 hours,

until the beans and chicos are tender. Stir the beans from time to time and make sure that there is enough liquid. Add the tomatoes and salt during the last half hour of cooking time.

5. Serve the chili inside a roasted acorn squash or with any of the grain dishes on pages 117–122. Garnish with chopped coriander and serve with shredded Monterey Jack and sour cream on the side.

YIELD: *6 to 8 servings*

VARIATIONS: As a substitute for chicos, use 2 cups of fresh or frozen corn kernels. You can make this a double corn chili by adding a 10-ounce package of frozen corn kernels to the above recipe. Add to the chili during the last half hour of cooking.

You can also substitute 1 cup of dried posole, soaked overnight, in place of the chicos.

In New Mexico and Arizona, dried corn (chicos) added to the chili pot will absorb excess liquid and at the same time give chili a distinctive regional overtone. Fresh corn, scraped from the cob, also brings a wonderful flavor to chili, but doesn't absorb as much liquid as dried corn.

—BILL BRIDGES, *The Great Chili Book*

Native Americans ate corn and beans together at almost every meal and planted them together in the same hill of earth, emphasizing the intimate culinary and nutritional relationship they have always shared.

—ELISABETH ROZIN, *Blue Corn and Chocolate*

> Other fruits and vegetables provide a meal and pass from memory. Not [chile] peppers. They grab the senses. They make us laugh. They make us cry. They make us think. They make us remember. They connect us to other people. They make us feel human. They make us feel alive.
>
> —SUSAN HAZEN-HAMMOND, *Chile Pepper Fever*

Vegetarian White Bean Chili

This is as far away as chili gets from the traditional meat lover's "bowl of red." It is an elegant, low-fat, vegetarian chili with a hint of mysterious smoky flavor from the chile chipotle. Serve it with a pilaf of brown and wild rice (page 120) and a big green salad, for a low-on-the-food-chain, politically correct, high complex-carbohydrate meal that will still satisfy even your most carnivorous guest.

- 4 tablespoons olive oil
- 6 pounds large yellow onions, peeled and coarsely chopped
- 6 large carrots, peeled and coarsely chopped
- 6 celery ribs, trimmed and coarsely chopped
- 8 garlic cloves, finely chopped or pushed through a garlic press
- 6 green Poblano, New Mexico, or Anaheim chiles, roasted, peeled, seeded, and finely chopped (see directions on page 45), or 2 cans (4 ounces each) chopped mild green chiles
- 2 to 3 fresh jalapeño peppers, seeded and finely chopped
- 1 to 2 chiles chipotle in adobo sauce, finely minced (optional)
- 4 large ripe tomatoes, peeled, seeded, and coarsely chopped, or 1 can (28 ounces) whole tomatoes, drained and coarsely chopped
- 1 bunch parsley, finely chopped
- 2 tablespoons whole cumin seeds, toasted
- 1 tablespoon dried oregano
- 1 teaspoon dried thyme
- 4 cups white beans, soaked 6 hours or overnight (see instructions on page 84)
- 3 quarts vegetable broth (page 62), chicken broth, or water.
- 1 tablespoon freshly ground black pepper, or to taste
- 2 bay leaves
- Salt, to taste

- 1 cup finely chopped cilantro
- 1 tablespoon fresh thyme leaves

1. Heat the olive oil in a large pot over medium heat. Sauté the onions, carrots, and celery for 10 to 15 minutes. Add the garlic and chiles and sauté, stirring, for 2 minutes longer. Stir in tomatoes, parsley, cumin, oregano, and thyme.
2. Drain the beans and add them together with 2½ quarts of the broth or water to the pot with the vegetables. Add black pepper and bay leaves.
3. Simmer, uncovered, over low heat, for 2½ to 3 hours, until beans are tender and the chili has thickened. Check the chili frequently while it is cooking and add more broth or water if necessary. Season with salt and pepper to taste. Add more chile chipotle if you like it hotter. Stir in chopped cilantro and fresh thyme leaves. Remove bay leaves and serve. Serve with Brown Rice Pilaf (page 120), Pico de Gallo Salsa (page 112), and a bowl of freshly grated Monterey Jack cheese.

YIELD: *12 to 14 servings*

Sag Harbor's Vegetarian Chili

> Do you suffer from yellow fever? Malaria? Kidney failure? Apoplexy? Cancer? Heart Disease? Spring fever? The common cold? Have you been rejected in love? Has a witch put a hex on you? Do you have the seven-year itch? Are your fingers swollen and twisted with arthritis? Do you suffer from one intense headache after another, day after day? Would you like to lose weight? Or perhaps you're reading this in the middle of childbirth and find that, although you've been in labor for hours, the baby still hasn't come?
>
> The cure, my friends, is always the same. Peppers. Peppers. Peppers. Eat them. Breathe them. Rub them on your skin. And like some Biblical sufferer, you'll be able to take up your bed and walk and be whole again.
>
> —SUSAN HAZEN-HAMMOND, *Chile Pepper Fever*

The Provisions Health Food Store and Café, in the historic whaling village of Sag Harbor, is also a local center of art and music, and a great place to shop, meet one's friends, and generally hang out. Their terrific vegetarian chili is always on the menu and I've enjoyed it for years.

- 3 cups red kidney beans, soaked for 6 hours or overnight, (see instructions on page 84), or 4 cans (15 ounces) red kidney beans, rinsed and drained
- 3 tablespoons olive oil
- 3 large onions, coarsely chopped
- 4 tablespoons minced garlic (about 20 medium cloves)
- 1 can (14½ ounces) crushed tomatoes
- 1 large carrot, diced
- 1 celery rib, diced
- 1 large baking potato, peeled, cut into ½-inch cubes, and covered with water
- 1 large yam, peeled, cut into ½-inch cubes, and covered with water
- 2 to 4 tablespoons chili powder (homemade or a good commercial brand)
- 2 tablespoons tamari soy sauce
- 1 bay leaf
- 2 teaspoons dried oregano
- 2 teaspoons dried basil
- 2 teaspoons dried marjoram
- 2 teaspoons dried thyme
- 1 teaspoon ground coriander
- 1 teaspoon ground cumin
- Salt and freshly ground black pepper, to taste

1 cup tomato juice
1 cup TVP (textured vegetable protein)*
Tabasco sauce, to taste

> **Eating chiles will make your head so soft, you'll believe anything.**
>
> —H. ALLEN SMITH, quoted in *Chile Pepper Fever*

1. Drain the beans and place them in a large heavy pot. Add enough water to cover by 2 inches and bring to a boil. Lower the heat and simmer, uncovered, for 1½ to 2 hours, until the beans are tender.
2. Heat the olive oil in a large heavy pot over medium heat. Add the onions and sauté, stirring, for 5 to 10 minutes, until onions are soft. Add the garlic and cook, stirring, for 2 minutes. Add the tomatoes, carrot, celery, potato, yam, chili powder, tamari, bay leaf, and all the herbs. Stir well, cover the pot, and cook over medium-low heat for 20 to 25 minutes, until the vegetables are tender.
3. Add the beans, salt, pepper, and a little water if necessary, and cook for 30 minutes longer. Add the tomato juice and TVP. Continue cooking for a few minutes over medium heat. The TVP needs not to cook but to fully absorb the liquid and to soften. The chili is done when the TVP is soft and piping hot. Taste and adjust the seasoning with salt, pepper, and few dashes of Tabasco sauce. Serve with corn bread (page 96–102) on the side.

YIELD: *8 to 10 servings*

*TVP (textured vegetable protein) is a protein extract of soybeans that has been formulated into flakes and dried. It is added to dishes as a protein supplement and a meat replacement. It is extremely nutritious, 70 percent to 90 percent protein, and very low in fat. The flavor is very bland and takes on the taste of the dish in which it is reconstituted.

A [chile] pepper eater doesn't simply like the bite of the pepper: he yearns for it. He may look forward to a meal to satisfy his hunger, but it's the prospect of the pepper accompanying his every bite that cheers him and makes eating a new indulgence every time. The pepper gives a certain sensory dimension to his dish, however elaborate and delicate the food might already be. The pepper accents his entire culinary existence.

—AMAL NAJ, *Peppers: A Story of Hot Pursuits*

Tofu in Red Chile Sauce

In this recipe, adapted from one I found in a book called Hot and Spicy and Meatless, the tofu replaces the meat to make a delicious and unusual vegetarian chili. If you are not a strict vegetarian, I suggest you use a good homemade chicken broth instead of the vegetable stock, for a richer flavor.

- 4 pounds (4 packages) firm tofu
- ¼ cup olive oil
- 1 large onion, coarsely chopped
- 4 large garlic cloves, coarsely chopped
- ¼ cup mild New Mexico chile powder
- ¼ cup ancho chile powder
- 1 chile chipotle in adobo sauce, finely diced
- 1 teaspoon ground coriander
- 1 teaspoon Mexican oregano, pulverized between your fingers
- 1 teaspoon toasted, ground cumin
- 1 tablespoon honey
- 2 tablespoon balsamic vinegar
- 2 tablespoons tamari soy sauce
- ¼ cup roasted pumpkin seeds
- 2 cups vegetable broth (page 62) or chicken broth

1. Slice the blocks of tofu lengthwise and place the slices between layers of paper towels. Place large books, heavy pots, or any other weighty object of your choice on the tofu to press out the excess liquid. Let the weighted tofu sit for 15 to 20 minutes.
2. Slice the tofu into ½-inch cubes. Heat the olive oil in a large heavy skillet over medium-high heat until it is hot but not smoking. Add the tofu cubes and sauté until the tofu is golden brown. Remove with a slotted spoon and drain on paper towels. Place the tofu in a glass or ceramic bowl and set aside.
3. Remove all but 1 tablespoon of the olive oil from the skillet. Add the onion and garlic and sauté over medium-high heat for about 5 minutes, until the onion has softened.

Lower the heat, add the chile powders and the diced chile chipotle, and cook, stirring, for 5 minutes longer. Stir in coriander, oregano, cumin, honey, vinegar, and soy sauce. Cook, stirring, for 1 minute and remove from heat.

4. Place the pumpkin seeds in the bowl of a food processor or blender and process until they are pulverized. Add 1 cup of broth and process to blend. Add onion-chile mixture from the skillet and process to blend.
5. Place the mixture in a large saucepan, add the remaining broth, and heat through. Gently stir in the tofu cubes, remove from heat, and let the tofu marinate at room temperature for 1 to 2 hours.
6. Bring the marinating tofu to a boil, reduce heat to low, and simmer, partially covered, for 1 hour. Serve over Brown Rice Pilaf (page 120) with Red Onion Salsa (page 110) or Hot Green Chile Salsa (page 114) on the side.

YIELD: *6 to 8 servings*

Peppers are a food with a following—the superstar of the garden, with organized fans (aficionados), fan clubs, T-shirts, mascots—the works, not just casual admirers. They have been called a good-time food, one you look forward to eating. Just thinking about them is exciting!

—JEAN ANDREWS, *Peppers*

Chile con Tempeh

Although tempeh is a fairly new ingredient in our culture, it is an ancient food in Indonesia. It is made from hulled soybeans, fermented by a mold that imparts a particular flavor and texture. It is very high in protein and vitamins and very low in fat. Its slightly crunchy and chewy texture makes it a very popular substitute for meat. Look for it in the refrigerated section of your health food store.

This chili is not only completely virtuous, delicious, and satisfying, but also can be prepared in under half an hour.

- 2 tablespoons olive oil
- 8 ounces (1 package) tempeh, cut into 1-inch pieces
- 1 large onion, coarsely chopped
- 4 garlic cloves, finely minced
- 6 large mushroom caps (shiitake, cremini, or cultivated white), thinly sliced
- 2 tablespoons mild New Mexico chile powder
- 2 tablespoons ancho chile powder
- 1 teaspoon toasted, ground cumin
- 1 cup coarsely chopped, drained, canned tomatoes
- 3 carrots, cut into ½-inch chunks
- 2 celery ribs, cut into ½-inch chunks
- 3 cups vegetable broth (page 62) or water
- 2 cups cooked red kidney beans, or 1 can (15 ounces) red kidney beans, drained and rinsed
- ¼ cup bulgur
- Salt, to taste
- Cayenne, to taste

1. Heat 1 tablespoon of the olive oil in a heavy skillet over medium heat until hot but not smoking. Sauté the tempeh until it is lightly browned on both sides. Remove the tempeh to paper towels and reserve.
2. Heat the remaining oil in a heavy pot and sauté the onion and garlic for 5 minutes, until the onion is softened. Add the sliced mushrooms and sauté for 3 minutes longer. Stir in the chile powders and cumin and sauté for 3 more minutes.

3. Add the tomatoes, carrots, celery, vegetable broth or water, kidney beans, bulgur, and tempeh. Stir the chili and bring it to a boil, reduce heat to a simmer, and cook for 20 to 25 minutes, until the chili has thickened. Taste and add salt and cayenne to your liking. Serve in bowls over Brown Rice Pilaf (page 120).

YIELD: *6 servings*

> I decided a long time ago that I like chili, but not enough to argue about it with people from Texas.
> —CALVIN TRILLIN, *American Fried*

Many Vegetable Vegetarian Chili

This chili features a selection of vegetables, with beans and bulgur playing a supporting role. It is the kind of recipe to which other vegetables such as yams or sweet potatoes, pumpkin or butternut squash, chick-peas or even lentils could easily be added. Let your taste and whatever you happen to have on hand be your guide.

- 1 spaghetti squash (weighing 3 to 4 pounds), scrubbed clean and rubbed with vegetable oil
- 2 tablespoons olive oil
- 2 large onions, coarsely chopped
- 6 large garlic cloves, finely chopped
- 2 large carrots, peeled and cut into ¼-inch dice
- 2 celery ribs, slit in half lengthwise and cut into ½-inch rounds
- 2 red bell peppers, cored, seeded, and diced
- 2 small zucchini,
- ½ pound mushrooms, wiped clean and cut into thin slices
- 3 to 4 tablespoons chili powder homemade (or a good commercial brand)
- 1 can (28 ounces) tomatoes, coarsely chopped with their juices
- 2 cups corn kernels, cut from 4 ears of corn, or 1 package thawed, frozen corn kernels
- 2 cups vegetable or chicken broth
- ½ cup bulgur
- 2 cups cooked pinto, red kidney, or black beans, or 1 can (15 ounces), drained and rinsed

1. Preheat the oven to 350° F. When the oven is ready, place the squash on the middle rack of the oven and bake for 45 to 50 minutes, until the squash begins to give and feels tender when pressed.
2. While the squash is baking, heat the olive oil in a large casserole or Dutch oven over medium-high heat, until it

is hot but not smoking. Add the onions, garlic, carrots, celery, bell peppers, zucchini, and mushrooms. Stir well and cover the pot to let the vegetables sweat for 10 minutes, until they have softened.

3. Uncover the pot and add the chili powder. Cook, stirring, for 3 minutes. Add the tomatoes, corn kernels, vegetable or chicken broth, and bulgur and mix well. Reduce heat to low and simmer, uncovered, for 45 minutes. Stir in the beans and simmer for 15 minutes longer.
4. Remove the squash from the oven and cut it in half lengthwise. When it is cool enough to handle, scrape out the seeds with a spoon and discard. Use a fork to scrape out the flesh into spaghetti-like strands. Stir the spaghetti squash into the chili and serve over polenta or rice (pages 117–122) and pass a bowl of Tomatillo Salsa (page 113) or Hot Green Chile Salsa (page 114).

YIELD: *6 servings*

A meat eater could live on beans and never miss meat. When a Mexican laborer is unable to lift a heavy weight, his companions say he "lacks frijoles." As you may deduce, I am a kind of frijole man. On the oldtime ranches of the border country, where I grew up, frijoles were about as regular as bread, and in some households they still are.

—J. FRANK DOBIE, *A Taste of Texas*

SALSA
CABBAGE
SLAW
CHEESE
CORN BREAD
CORN
CHIPS
RICE
TOMATO
TORTILLAS
SOUR
CREAM
AVOCADOS
CHILI
COMPANIONS

The table at an old-timer's chili party would probably have a pot of beans beside the chili, for those who like them, plus a large bowl of freshly chopped onion; a small bowl of dried red chilipiquins; a fresh bright-red bottle of Tabasco sauce; yellow pickled "eating" chiles; crackers—preferably the little "chili" crackers—and plenty of cold beer.

—BILL BRIDGES,
The Great Chili Book

Beans

If pale beans bubble for you in a red earthenware pot
You can oft decline the dinners of sumptuous hosts.

—MARTIAL,
a Roman poet writing nearly two thousand years ago,
quoted in *The Home Book of Quotations*

About Beans

Anasazi beans: The word "Anasazi" means "the old ones," and refers to the founder of Pueblo culture in the fifth century AD. This native American bean was cultivated at that time and is considered to be one of the oldest existing beans in the Southwest. The color is a deep maroon speckled with white and it is about the same size as a pinto bean. It has an excellent, slightly sweet flavor, with an almost chocolate aroma. Although I have never met a bean I didn't like, this is one of my all-time favorites. It is not commonly found in markets outside the Southwest, but it can be purchased through mail-order sources, and you might find it in a well-stocked health food store.

Black beans: Also known as black turtle beans, they are small, kidney-shaped, and dark purple to black in color. They have an earthy, slightly sweet taste that goes well with strongly flavored meat such as venison or lamb, and they can hold their own in a vegetarian dish as well.

Kidney beans: Kidney beans come in lots of sizes and colors, but the most popular kidney bean for chili is the beautiful red kidney bean. It has a nice "fat" taste and holds its shape and color very well.

Pinto beans: Deep reddish brown markings on a pink background inspired the Spanish to call these beans *pinto* (painted). The bean of choice throughout the Southwest for satisfying eating at breakfast, lunch, and dinner.

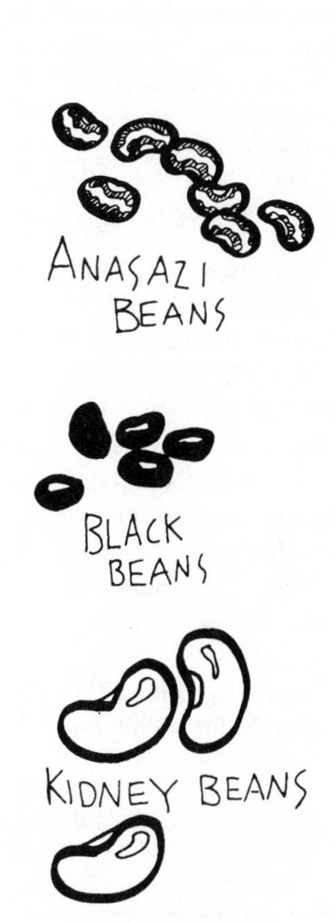

When you have four hundred pounds of beans in the house, you need have no fear of starvation. Other things, delicacies such as sugar, tomatoes, peppers, coffee, fish or meat may come sometimes miraculously, through the intercession of the Virgin, sometimes through industry or cleverness; but your beans are there, and you are safe.
—JOHN STEINBECK, *Tortilla Flat*

The pinto bean is hard to beat, with dry salt in the pot. Frijoles? Well it's jes' the same, jes' give me what y'u've got. Now jes' in case yore beans is white, knowed as the navy sort, I'll take a helpin' jes the same, about a half a quart. Or if yore beans is big an' red an' sort of kidney shape, I'll go along besides the fire an' fill my ole tin plate.
—TEX TAYLOR, quoted in *Come an' Get It: The Story of the Old Cowboy Cook*

White beans: This category includes navy beans, Great Northern, cannellini, and white kidney. They all have a lovely creamy texture when cooked.

WHITE CANNELLINI BEANS

Some Basic Facts About Cooking Beans

1. I urge you to take the trouble to search out beans from the current year's crop. Old beans (more than a year old) become drier and harder as they age, need to soak longer because they have to absorb more water, and can take a *long* time to cook. There is also some loss of flavor, but nutritionally they are as good as new. Try to buy organically grown beans of the most current crop.
2. It is handy to know that 1 pound of dried beans is made up of about 2 cups, and when they are cooked, you will have 4 or 5 cups of cooked beans. Another rule of thumb is to use 1 teaspoon salt per 1 cup dry beans, less if cooking with salty meat or stock.
3. Pick over the beans to remove any grit or stones, and wash them in several changes of cold water.
4. To soak or not to soak? Probably because I enjoy slow-paced cooking, I usually soak my beans, leaving them to stand overnight, or all day long if I put them up to soak in the morning. During the soaking I change the water three or four times, because this eliminates some of the gas-producing substances in the beans. If you prefer not to soak them overnight, here is a quick-soak method that works extremely well. Pick over and wash the beans. Place them in a large pot with enough water to cover by 2 or 3 inches. Bring the beans to a boil and let them boil for about 3 minutes. Turn off the heat, cover the pot, and let

stand for 1 or 2 hours. Drain the beans and cover with fresh, cold water by at least two inches and proceed with the cooking.

5. Beans should be cooked slowly, at a gentle simmer, to keep them from becoming tough. Do not undercook the beans. To my mind, cooked beans should never have anything crunchy about them. They should be soft and meltingly tender, which will also make them easier to digest. Most beans take anywhere between 2 and 3 hours to reach this point, and I have known beans to take somewhat longer. Never add salt, tomatoes, vinegar, or any other acidic ingredients until the last half hour of cooking, or your beans will never get tender.
6. Store cooked beans, tightly covered, in the refrigerator for up to 5 days. Freeze cooked beans in pint containers for several months.

There is much to be said for the succulent little bean—any kind of a bean, be it kidney, navy, green, wax, Kentucky, chili, baked, pinto, Mexican, or any other kind. Not only is it high in nourishment, but it is particularly rich in that nutritious value referred to as protein—the stuff that imparts energy and drive to the bean eater and particularly senators who need this sustaining force when they prepare for a long speech on the Senate floor.

—SENATOR EVERETT DIRKSON, "Homage to the Bean," *The Complete Bean Cookbook*

> Most cooks prefer the pinto bean which takes its name from the brown spots on its surface. Some like the navy bean, some the red, but any are good if cooked right. The cowman knew nothing of proteins, minerals, and vitamins, but he did know that the lowly bean satisfied his hunger, was easy to keep, easy to cook, and cheap. The sight of a black iron pot half full of beans cooking, its miniature geysers throwing up little jets of steam with a *plop, plop,* as it bubbled away over a slow fire would excite any man's appetite.
>
> —RAMON F. ADAMS, *Come an' Get It: The Story of the Old Cowboy Cook*

Cowboy Beans

This is one of the most basic recipes for beans I have come across. It is so basic, you don't even have to remember the ingredients, because in a pinch you can leave out the bacon or pork and simply add a tablespoon or two of flavorful olive oil.

You can serve these with any chili, either on the side, underneath, or mixed into the chili. If you don't have any chili to serve them with, you can do what J. Frank Dobie advised: Crush 3 chiltecpins into each serving of beans and top with a tablespoon of raw onion and a sprinkling of vinegar. The chiltecpins are very hot, so you might prefer to start with just one or even half of one, but they are very flavorful and the heat is of a surprisingly brief duration. Or, you can mash a couple of green roasted and peeled chiles into your bowl of beans; or, chop up a chile chipotle in adobo sauce and stir that into your beans; top with some chopped raw onions and some grated Jack cheese and you've still got a most satisfying meal.

2 cups (1 pound) dried pinto beans
4 bacon slices, finely diced, or ¼ cup finely diced salt pork
Salt and freshly ground black pepper, to taste

1. Pick over the beans to remove any foreign objects. Wash the beans and soak them in plenty of cold water for at least 6 hours or overnight, changing the water several times.
2. Drain the beans and place them together with the bacon in a large pot with enough cold water to cover by at least 2 inches. Simmer, uncovered, for 3 hours, until beans are very tender. Add more water as needed so the beans do not burn. Add salt and pepper to taste and simmer for 30 minutes longer.

YIELD: *about 4½ cups cooked beans*

Chili Beans

Another variation of basic stewed beans is this Tex-Mex dish. It adds, in its simplest version, red chiles and tomatoes to the beans, and makes a great side dish to roasted or grilled meats and chicken. Make it a day ahead for even better flavor.

2 cups (1 pound) dried pinto beans
1 medium onion, finely chopped
4 garlic cloves, finely chopped
2 tablespoons brown sugar
1 teaspoon toasted cumin seed
1 teaspoon Mexican oregano
2 bay leaves
¼ cup finely chopped salt pork
2 cups canned tomatoes, drained and coarsely chopped
2 tablespoons cider vinegar
4 tablespoons mild New Mexico chile powder
1 teaspoon cayenne, or to taste
Salt, to taste
Freshly ground black pepper, to taste

1. Pick over the beans to remove any foreign objects. Wash the beans and soak them in cold water for at least 6 hours or overnight, changing the water several times.
2. Place the beans in a large ovenproof pot or Dutch oven and add enough cold water to cover by 2 inches. Bring to a boil and reduce heat to low. Add the onion, garlic, brown sugar, cumin seed, oregano, and bay leaves. Simmer, uncovered, for 2 hours. Add more water as needed so the beans do not burn.
3. Preheat the oven to 325° F.
4. Add the salt pork, tomatoes, cider vinegar, chile powder, cayenne, salt, and freshly ground black pepper. Stir well and make sure there is enough liquid to cover the beans by about 1 inch. Cover and bake at 325° F. for 45 minutes to 1 hour. The beans should be very tender, with their liquid thickened to a sauce. Taste and adjust the seasoning.

YIELD: *4 to 6 servings*

She pointed to the flushed and irritable children. See, they were all sick. They were not getting the proper food. "What is the proper food?" Pilon demanded. "Beans," she said. "There you have something to trust, something that will not go right through you."
—JOHN STEINBECK, *Tortilla Flat*

Pintos, also called West Texas or Pecos strawberries, are a stimulus to the cook's creativity. A basic recipe calls for about three cups of beans to feed a dozen people. They may be soaked overnight and cooked four to six hours the next day. It is still customary in many homes in Texas to start the beans before the coffeepot is put on the stove for breakfast.

—ERNESTINE LINCK AND JOYCE ROACH, *Eats: A Folk History of Texas Foods*

Stewed Pinto Beans

Stewed pinto beans, sometimes called by their Spanish name, frijoles, are a staple throughout the Southwest and a basic component of Tex-Mex cooking wherever it is served. A tiny town called Dove Creek in southwestern Colorado calls itself "The Pinto Bean Center of the World" because it grows so many pinto beans. But pintos are raised in great quantities all over New Mexico, Arizona, Texas, and even parts of Nebraska.

I think that the most basic recipe I have come across involves simply stewing the beans in water and throwing in a little salt at the end. Gradually I've added other ingredients that enhance the beans but do not overpower them. A bit of sugar might seems strange but actually brings out the natural sweetness of pinto beans.

- 2 cups (1 pound) dried pinto beans
- 1 medium onion, finely chopped
- 3 garlic cloves, finely minced
- 2 bay leaves
- 1 teaspoon sugar
- 2 teaspoons salt
- ½ cup finely minced salt pork, or 2 tablespoons bacon drippings (optional)

1. Pick over the beans to remove any foreign objects. Wash the beans and soak them in plenty of cold water for at least 6 hours or overnight, changing the water several times.
2. Place the beans in a large pot and add enough cold water to cover by 2 inches.
3. Bring to a boil and reduce heat to low. Add the onion, garlic, bay leaves, and sugar. Simmer, uncovered, for 3 hours, until beans are very tender. Add more water as needed so the beans do not burn.
4. Add the salt and salt pork or bacon drippings, if using, and simmer, uncovered, for 30 minutes longer.

YIELD: *about 4½ cups cooked beans*

VARIATION: Substitute any other beans—Anasazi, kidney, white, or black turtle beans, or even a mixture of beans—for the pintos. In my experience, black beans sometimes take much longer to cook until tender, sometimes 5 or 6 hours. Keep adding water to the pot so they don't burn, and cook until they are tender.

Pinto beans served to our banker persuaded him not to foreclose our mortgage.

—ANNALEY REDD,
as quoted in *Trail Boss's Cowboy Cookbook*

There's a legend in the Southwest that says in order for a man to start a cow ranch he needs only three items: a sourdough starter, jerky line, and a bean pot.

The beans for the pot are frijoles, a Mexican word for beans . . . Even when a tenderfoot calls them "fry-joles" a southwesterner knows what he means. But any way you say it, just plain beans means only one kind, and that is the spotted brown-and-white pinto bean.

—STELLA HUGHES, *Bacon & Beans, Ranch-Country Recipes*

Drunken Pinto Beans

Beer replaces some of the cooking water and adds a rich deep flavor to the beans. If you love beans, as I do, you will want to have them even when you are not eating chili. One of my favorite lunch or easy supper dishes is to mash them up with some roasted green chile (canned will do just fine), roll up in a warmed tortilla or spread on good crusty bread, top with a little salsa, hot sauce, or nothing at all, and enjoy.

- 2 cups (1 pound) dried pinto beans
- 1 bottle dark beer
- 1 large onion, coarsely chopped
- 2 garlic cloves, finely diced
- 2 jalapeño chiles, stems and seeds removed, finely diced
- 1 chile chipotle (dried, smoked jalapeño), soaked in hot water for 20 minutes, cut in half, stems and seeds removed
- 1 tablespoon olive oil
- 1 tablespoon salt, or to taste

1. Wash and sort the beans. Place them in a large pot and cover with plenty of cold water. Let the beans soak overnight, changing the water several times.
2. Drain the beans and put them back in the pot. Add the beer and enough water to cover the beans by 2 inches. Add the onion, garlic, fresh jalapeños, chile chipotle, and olive oil. Bring to a boil, reduce heat to low, and simmer, uncovered, for 2 to 3 hours.
3. Check on the beans from time to time and add more boiling water if necessary. After the beans have been cooking for about 2 hours and have begun to soften, add the salt and cook until completely tender.

YIELD: *about 4½ cups, serving 6 to 8 people*

VARIATION: Substitute any other beans—Anasazi, kidney, white, or black turtle beans, or even a mixture of beans—for the pintos. In my experience, black beans sometimes take much longer to cook until tender, sometimes 5 or 6 hours. Keep adding water to the pot so they don't burn, and cook until they are tender.

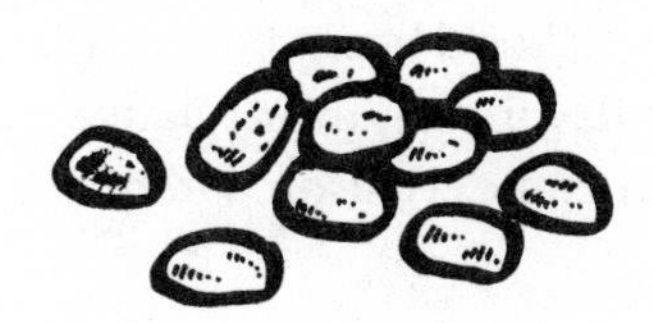

Domesticated beans predate corn and were tamed about 10,000 years ago in Peru and apparently moved north into Mexico and eventually Southwest and to the rest of the country. When the Europeans arrived, the common bean, *Phaseolus vulgaris,* was being grown everywhere in what is the United States. In the Southwest, another species, *P. acutifolius* or the tepary bean, was more popular because it was a rapid grower and resistant to drought and alkalinity. Black varieties of tepary beans, such as Mitla Black Bean, are used in the famous black bean soups.

—DAVE DEWITT AND MARY JANE WILAN, *The Food Lover's Handbook to the Southwest*

Black Beans

Black beans have become the darling of many of today's chefs, who are cooking with native American ingredients and are, in a sense, reinventing American regional cuisine. There is nothing surprising about their embracing this member of *Phaseolus vulgaris,* the botanical family to which kidney, navy, pea, pinto, and other New World beans belong. Black beans have a somewhat heartier flavor than their relatives, and they marry especially well with game, venison, lamb, and well-seasoned beef.

- 2 cups (1 pound) dried black beans
- 2 tablespoons olive oil
- 1 large onion, diced
- 3 garlic cloves, minced
- 2 tablespoons toasted, ground cumin
- 3 sprigs fresh or dried epazote (optional)
- 1 tablespoon salt, or to taste

1. Pick over the beans to remove any foreign objects. Wash the beans and soak them in water for at least 6 hours or overnight, changing the water several times.
2. Heat the oil in a large heavy pot over low heat. Add the onion and garlic and cook, stirring, for 5 minutes, until the onion has wilted.
3. Drain the beans and add them to the onions and garlic, along with enough water to cover by 2 inches. Add the cumin and epazote, if using, and bring to a boil. Reduce heat to low and simmer, uncovered, for 3 hours or longer, until the beans are very tender. Stir the beans from time to time and make sure that there is enough liquid to cover them. Add salt during the last half hour of cooking.

YIELD: *about 4½ cups cooked beans*

VARIATION: Add a small ham hock to the beans while they are cooking for a haunting, delicious smoky flavor.

Refried Beans

Throughout the Southwest and even in California, this is one of the most popular of all side dishes and it can be found served with almost every meal, filling in at breakfast with eggs, warmed in a tortilla for lunch, or appearing as an hors d'oeuvre topped with grated cheese and surrounded by crispy corn chips at dinnertime.

Although the beans are called refried, they are in fact stewed beans that are then fried, only once, with more seasonings and in a flavorful fat such as bacon drippings, butter, or olive oil. If you want refried beans and don't have any cooked beans around, go ahead and use canned beans. The soft, canned texture doesn't matter because the beans are mashed, and this cooking method gives them a rich, full flavor.

- 4 tablespoons bacon drippings, butter, or olive oil
- 1 medium onion, finely chopped
- 2 to 3 garlic cloves, pushed through a garlic press
- ½ teaspoon cayenne
- ½ teaspoon freshly ground black pepper
- 4 cups cooked pinto beans in their cooking liquid (or any other cooked or canned beans, with their liquid)
- ½ cup freshly grated Monterey Jack (optional)
- Salt, to taste

1. Heat the bacon drippings, butter, or olive oil in a large heavy skillet over medium heat. Add the onion, garlic, cayenne, and black pepper. Lower the heat, cover the skillet, and cook for 5 minutes, until the onion is wilted.
2. Uncover the skillet, return heat to medium, and add the beans and their liquid. Use a potato masher to mash the beans. They can be partially mashed or entirely mashed, the texture is up to you. But they should be mashed well enough to absorb their cooking liquid. Continue cooking until the beans are heated through. Stir in the optional cheese and taste for seasoning. Adjust the seasoning, adding more salt, cayenne, and black pepper to taste.

YIELD: *4 to 6 servings*

No one has yet found a way, luckily, to botch the lowly bean the way wheat flour and white rice have been ruined. If a person is still interested in a food that is cheap, keeps indefinitely while in the dry state, is low in fat, high in protein, and improves in flavor each time it is reheated, he'll do well to stock up on sacks of pinto beans.

—STELLA HUGHES, *Bacon & Beans, Ranch-Country Recipes*

The refrito beans that are a specialty of Mexico today—boiled, mashed, fried and served with a topping of grated cheese—evolved only after the Spaniards introduced the cow and other domesticated animals to Central America. Before that, there seems to have been no reliable supply of fat or oil.

—REAY TANNAHILL, *Food in History*

Breads

> **The smell of good bread baking, like the sound of lightly flowing water, is indescribable in its evocation of innocence and delight.**
>
> —M.F.K. FISHER, quoted in *A Cook's Alphabet of Quotations*

About Corn Breads and Muffins

If you make chili, you will want to make corn bread. There is no chili in the world that doesn't taste better with some corn bread on the side. Fortunately, corn bread and muffins are among the easiest and most satisfying breads you can bake. They are so quick and so easy that you could have fresh hot corn bread or muffins with every meal and very little trouble on your part. This was, in fact, the case in many early American households.

I make most of my corn breads in a heavy black cast iron skillet that measures 9 inches in diameter (10 or even 12 inches in diameter would be fine, too). The skillet should always be preheated in the oven with some butter or oil so that the corn bread batter goes into a hot well-greased skillet. This method produces a bread that is crispy on the outside and light and moist inside. But corn breads are nothing if not adaptable, so if you don't own a heavy skillet or pan, or have mixed up your batter and forgotten to preheat the skillet, go ahead and bake the bread in an unheated buttered or oiled skillet or baking pan. Any baking pan approximately 8 x 8 x 2 inches is suitable to use instead of the 9-inch skillet. You can bake any corn bread recipe (except for spoon bread) as muffins or corn sticks, or vice versa.

The recipes are adaptable in many other ways as well. Yellow, white, and blue cornmeal are all interchangeable—only do try to get the freshest, organic stone-ground cornmeal (see mail-order sources on page 125) and keep it refrigerated. If buttermilk is called for and you don't have any on hand, substitute an equal amount of plain low-fat yogurt; or milk (skim or regular) plus 1 tablespoon lemon juice. No lemon in the house? Skip it; the bread will still come out okay. You can leave out or increase the amount of sugar called for. The taste for sugar in corn bread is personal as well as regional. Northerners tend to like their corn breads sweet; southerners never add sugar. You can add fresh herbs, a little bit of cheese, a handful of corn kernels, or some crumbled bacon bits to almost any corn bread recipe. If you are watching your cholesterol, substitute vegetable oil for butter, use two egg whites for every whole egg, substitute skim milk or buttermilk (very low in fat) for whole milk, and leave out any cheese.

Most of the recipes in this section can be made in about 30 minutes. You can turn any meal into a special occasion by serving hot corn bread fresh from the oven. For best flavor, try to serve corn bread as soon as possible after it is baked. Corn breads are not great keepers, so if you have leftovers, you can do as our forefathers did, crumble some stale corn bread into a soup bowl, pour in some milk (a little brown sugar is optional), and have yourself a great breakfast or snack.

For corn is the ultimate, the essential American food, the one that began here, the one that stayed here. Unlike many other New World foods that crossed the oceans to find new homes in a host of Old World cuisines, corn was accepted outside its ancestral home only in a few areas characterized by extreme poverty and deprivation—regions of rural Italy, Spain, and France, the Balkans, and much of sub-Saharan Africa.

—ELISABETH ROZIN, *Blue Corn and Chocolate*

Basic Skillet Corn Bread

One of the great things about corn bread is that you can have a hot, wonderfully aromatic bread on the table in less than 45 minutes, including the time it takes to preheat the oven. It is the natural companion to any chili in this book. Served with any of the vegetarian chilis, it complements the beans to make a complete protein.

This delicious corn bread gets very crisp on the outside and remains moist inside.

- 2 tablespoons unsalted butter
- 1½ cups buttermilk
- 2 large eggs
- 1 teaspoon salt
- 1 teaspoon baking powder
- ½ teaspoon baking soda
- 2 cups white or yellow cornmeal, preferably organic and stone-ground

1. Preheat the oven to 450° F.
2. Place the butter in a heavy cast iron skillet and put it in the oven to heat while you mix together the corn bread batter (about 10 minutes).
3. In a large mixing bowl, whisk together the buttermilk and eggs. Stir in salt, baking powder, and baking soda. Stir in the cornmeal to make a batter. Swirl the oil or melted butter to coat the sides of the skillet. Pour the batter into the hot skillet and shake the skillet to smooth the batter. Bake for 20 minutes, until it turns a golden brown and the edges recede from the sides of the pan.

YIELD: *6 to 8 servings*

Easy Corn Muffins

I have this recipe stuck to the door of my refrigerator to remind me how quick and easy these muffins are to make, even at a moment's notice. You can substitute ½ cup whole corn kernels for the cream-style corn, or toss in some blueberries or dried cranberries if you like.

- 1 cup yellow cornmeal, preferably stone-ground and organic
- 1 cup unbleached all-purpose flour
- 3 tablespoons sugar
- 1 tablespoon baking powder
- ½ teaspoon salt
- 1 cup buttermilk
- 1 large egg, lightly beaten
- 4 tablespoons unsalted butter, melted
- 1 cup cream-style corn

1. Preheat the oven to 400° F.
2. Line a 12-cup muffin tin with paper baking cups, or grease the insides of the muffin cups.
3. Combine the cornmeal, flour, sugar, baking powder, and salt in a bowl and whisk together.
4. In another bowl, whisk together the buttermilk, egg, and melted butter. Stir into the dry ingredients and stir in the cream-style corn.
5. Fill the muffin cups three-quarters full and bake for 20 to 25 minutes, until muffins are golden and a tester inserted in the center comes out clean. Remove the muffins from the tin and serve while they are still warm.

YIELD: *12 muffins*

And those who came were resolved to be Englishmen,
Gone to the world's end, but English every one.
And they ate the white corn kernels, parched in the sun,
And they knew it not, but they'd not be English again.

—STEPHEN VINCENT BENÉT,
Selected Works of Stephen Vincent Benét, Volume 1

Chiles seem to frighten otherwise brave people, who handle them hesitantly and worry that they'll be too hot. There is an easy one-word answer to that problem: balance. If you have given a dish too much heat, you can easily add a touch of maple syrup or honey or a chunk of sweet fruit like mango or papaya to soften or balance it. They will bring harmony and complexity to the finished dish.

—BOBBY FLAY, *Bobby Flay's Bold American Food*

Green Chile Corn Bread

This rich, custardy corn bread is an extravagant variation on the more spartan corn breads that usually accompany a bowl of chile. Try serving this with one of the drier chilies, like the No-Nonsense Bowl of Red on page 6. It is also very good for breakfast with a side of Stewed Pinto Beans, page 88.

- ½ pound unsalted butter, at room temperature, plus additional butter for the baking pan
- ½ cup sugar
- 4 eggs
- 1½ cups canned cream-style corn
- ½ cup (one 4-ounce can) roasted and peeled mild green chiles, coarsely chopped
- 1 fresh hot green chile (jalapeño or serrano), seeded and deveined, finely chopped
- ½ cup grated Monterey Jack cheese
- 1 cup all-purpose flour
- 1 cup yellow cornmeal, preferably organic, and stone-ground
- 2 tablespoons baking powder
- 1 teaspoon salt

1. Preheat the oven to 325° F. Butter a 9-inch square baking pan.
2. Cream together the butter and sugar in the bowl of an electric mixer. Beat in the eggs, one at a time, then stir in the corn, chiles, cheese, flour, cornmeal, baking powder, and salt.

3. Pour the mixture into the prepared pan and bake for about 1 hour, until the sides of the bread have pulled away from the pan and the top is firm and springy to the touch.
4. Remove from the oven and serve while still warm.

YIELD: *6 to 8 servings*

Heap high the farmer's wintry hoard!
Heap high the golden corn!
No richer gift has Autumn poured
From out her lavish horn!

—JOHN GREENLEAF WHITTIER, "The Corn Song," quoted in *The Harper Book of American Quotations*

They eat the Indian corn in a great variety of forms . . .

—FRANCES TROLLOPE, *Domestic Manners of the Americans*

Chile Carrot Corn Bread

Although not at all traditional, this is one of my favorite corn breads. The sweetness of the grated carrot enhances the flavor of the cornmeal and marries very nicely with the pungency of red chile.

- 1½ cups grated carrot
- 2 eggs
- 2 tablespoons canola oil
- ⅓ cup honey
- 2 cups buttermilk
- 2 tablespoons mild New Mexico chile powder
- ½ teaspoon salt
- 1 teaspoon baking soda
- 1 teaspoon baking powder
- 2 cups yellow cornmeal
- 1 tablespoon butter

1. Preheat the oven to 450° F.
2. In a bowl, combine the carrots, eggs, canola oil, honey, and buttermilk. Mix with a wooden spoon until well blended.
3. Stir in chile powder, salt, baking soda, and baking powder. Then stir in cornmeal and blend to make a batter.
4. Melt the butter in a heavy cast iron skillet and use a paper towel to distribute butter evenly over the inside of the skillet. Pour in batter and bake 25 to 30 minutes, until the mixture shrinks away from the sides of the skillet. Let cool in skillet for 15 to 20 minutes before serving.

YIELD: *6 to 8 servings*

Corn Sticks

Everybody loves corn sticks because you get lots of crunchy crust surrounding the corn bread inside. These are fun to serve at a party, and the recipe doubles easily. It is easier if you have two cast-iron corn stick molds for baking the corn sticks. Fortunately they are not very expensive.

1 cup buttermilk
1 large egg, lightly beaten
2 tablespoons vegetable oil
2 tablespoons sugar
½ teaspoon baking soda
½ teaspoon baking powder
½ teaspoon salt
½ teaspoon cayenne (optional)
½ cup all-purpose flour
1 cup white cornmeal

1. Preheat the oven to 450° F.
2. Rub cast-iron corn stick molds (these should be 5½ inches long) with vegetable oil, or spray with spray release and preheat them in the hot oven while you are mixing the batter, for about 10 minutes. They should be very hot.
3. In a large mixing bowl, whisk together the buttermilk, egg, and vegetable oil. Stir in sugar, baking soda, baking powder, salt, and optional cayenne. Stir in flour and cornmeal to make a smooth batter.
4. Remove hot molds from the oven and spoon the batter into the molds, filling them about half full. Bake for about 15 minutes, or until corn sticks are golden brown. Slide corn sticks from mold and serve warm with plenty of butter.

YIELD: *14 corn sticks*

Planting was sacred and performed in association with vehement dancing for fertility. In many tribes the women would shake their long hair to encourage the magically similar corn silks to flourish. In Central America, Aztec ceremonies at corn planting included human sacrifice, serpentine dances, skirmishes among priestesses, and a rattle-strewing rite, where the rattle imitated the seed tumbling into the earth. The Green Corn Dance of the Pueblo Indians of the southwestern United States is a survival of ancient customs such as these, and is still performed today.

—MARGARET VISSER, *Much Depends on Dinner*

Corn for the Indian was both One and Various. Its many colours—orange, white, blue, black, and the rest—seemed to him the many faceted manifestation of the single and divine sap of *maïs*. There was a deep obligation to preserve its variety. The Hopi Indians allotted to each family in a village one type of corn, and it was that family's responsibility to maintain the purity of that corn type through the generations. In other words, hybridization, the core of the modern development of corn, would have been anathema to the Indians: hybridization confuses categories, refuses priorities, and denies the aspect of Many to what was One.

—MARGARET VISSER, *Much Depends on Dinner*

Piñon Corn Bread

Pine nuts, or piñones, are a native crop of Southwestern Pueblo Indians. The small, evergreen piñon trees thrive at elevations above 5,000 feet and are found all over the Southwest. The pine nuts ripen in the pine cones of these trees and are hand-gathered in the wild. These native pine nuts have a much stronger flavor than the nuts imported from either Italy or Greece, and are worth seeking out through mail-order sources.

In this recipe pine nuts are a perfect complement to the other flavors in the corn bread.

1½ cups pine nuts
2 cups blue cornmeal*
2 cups all-purpose flour
¼ cup sugar
3 tablespoons baking powder
2 teaspoons salt
½ teaspoon cayenne
2 cups milk
12 tablespoons (1½ sticks) unsalted butter, melted
2 eggs, lightly beaten
½ cup honey

1. Preheat the oven to 400° F.
2. Lightly grease a 13 x 9 x 2-inch baking pan.
3. Spread the pine nuts in a large heavy skillet and toast them over medium-high heat, stirring frequently, for about 5 minutes, until they start to turn a golden color. Be very careful not to avert your eyes even briefly for they can burn in a flash. Remove them to paper towels and let them cool.
4. In a large bowl, combine the cornmeal, flour, sugar, baking

*Blue cornmeal has a softer, less starchy texture than either yellow or white cornmeal, as well as slightly more flavor. You can purchase it through the mail from sources supplying other southwestern ingredients (page 125). You can also substitute yellow or white cornmeal in any recipe calling for blue cornmeal.

powder, salt, and cayenne. Stir with a wire whisk to mix well. Stir in the cooled pine nuts.

5. In another bowl, mix together the milk, butter, eggs, and honey. Stir the dry ingredients into the milk and butter mixture to make a batter.
6. Pour the batter into the prepared baking pan and bake for about 30 minutes, until the bread has started to pull away from the sides of the pan and a tester inserted into the center comes out clean. Serve while still warm.

YIELD: *16 to 20 servings*

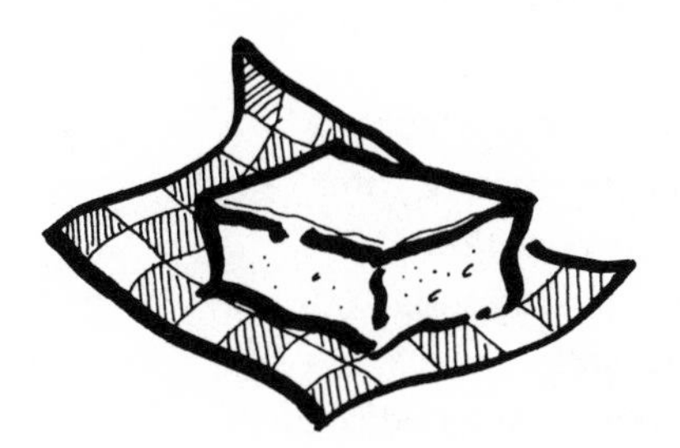

> Nuts from the piñon, a native low-growing pine, were used in salads and ground into paste for moles. The piñon wood itself warms the cold desert nights, and as cooking fuel, it imbues meats and fowl with an elusive piney flavor. There is a lovely local [Southwest] habit of lighting a small green piñon branch and walking it through the house, scenting the air more gently than any scented candle ever could.
>
> —CHRISTOPHER IDONE, *Glorious American Food*

> There are cooks that kin cook; there are cooks that cannot, an' it's a lucky outfit that knows when it's got for its wagon a cook that kin cook up a stew, some biscuits of sourdough, an' frijoles too. Now when our ole Cookie gits through with his cookin' he yells, "Come an' git it," an' sits back a-lookin'. He's techy by now, don't make no remarks, jes' fall to an' eat it like starved medder larks.
>
> —TEX TAYLOR, quoted in *Come an' Get It: The Story of the Old Cowboy Cook*

Sourdough Biscuits

In his charming book *Come an' Get It: The Story of the Old Cowboy Cook,* Ramon Adams writes that "One of the most famous of all Western foods was perhaps the sourdough biscuits of the range cook. No one seems to know who first created them, but they became a standard of the ranch country." Indeed, sourdough biscuits, fresh and hot from the oven, make a happy accompaniment to a bowl of chili. And although cowboys on the trail expected these biscuits at nearly ever meal, today their appearance at the dinner table always turns any meal into a special occasion.

- 1 cup sourdough starter
- 4 cups nonchlorinated water
- 12 cups all-purpose flour
- 2 teaspoons baking soda
- 2 teaspoons salt
- 2 tablespoons granulated sugar
- ½ pound (2 sticks) unsalted butter
- 1 tablespoon vegetable oil

1. In a large (1 gallon or larger) bowl, combine the starter with nonchlorinated water and stir in 5 cups of the flour. Mix well with a wooden spoon, but don't worry if the mixture is somewhat lumpy. Cover with a towel and let stand overnight.
2. In the morning, stir in baking soda, salt, sugar, and 1 cup flour. Melt half the butter and beat into the dough until well mixed. (You can do this using the dough hook in your Kitchen Aid.)
3. Add the remaining flour, beating it in ½ cup at a time, until the dough becomes too stiff to beat. Turn out on a lightly floured surface and knead the dough until it is smooth and resilient. Form the dough into a ball and rub with the vegetable oil. Place it in a clean bowl, cover with a towel, and let rise in a warm place until doubled in bulk, 1½ to 2 hours.
4. Melt the remaining stick of butter and brush it on three

14 × 17-inch baking sheets. Reserve leftover melted butter for brushing on biscuits.

5. Preheat the oven to 375° F.
6. Punch down the risen dough and turn it out onto a lightly floured surface. Knead it briefly and divide the dough into 4 equal parts. Roll out one quarter of the dough at a time to a thickness of about ½ inch. Cut out biscuits with a 2- or 3-inch cookie cutter, dusted with flour before each cut.
7. Arrange biscuits so they are touching each other on prepared baking sheets (20 to each baking sheet) and brush the tops with remaining melted butter.
8. Bake for 20 to 25 minutes, or until they are a light golden color. Cool for 10 minutes on the baking sheets and remove to wire racks to cool completely. If you cannot bake them all at once, cover the waiting biscuits with a tea towel until they are ready to go into the oven.

YIELD: *40 to 60 biscuits, depending on size*

NOTE: You can use a commercial sourdough starter or make your own. To make your own, dissolve 1 tablespoon active dry yeast in ½ cup warm nonchlorinated water. Add 2 more cups warm nonchlorinated water and stir in 2½ cups unbleached white flour. If you can get organic flour, all the better. Cover and let stand in a draft-free place for 3 days.

Stir the mixture and refrigerate until ready to use. To keep the starter going, add ½ cup flour and ½ cup water every 5 days. Each time you use the starter, reserve at least 1 cup and replace what you have taken out with equal amounts of flour and water.

> Some sort of fry-bread is common among many of the tribes in the Southwest, but a traveller is most likely to meet up with it, as I first did, on Jeep tours through the Navajo reservation. . . . Cooked out of doors by shepherd families, where it is handpatted and fried in Dutch ovens over a juniper fire, the bread is in its true element. It emerges knobby, puffed and heavy in texture, needing nothing more than a bowl of green chili stew to make an outdoorsman's meal.
> —HUNTLEY DENT, *The Feast of Santa Fe*

Navajo Fry Bread

All over the Southwest, at fairs, pueblos, festivals, and rodeos, you will find Native American women selling fry bread hot out of their frying pans. Most often people simply eat it out of hand to satisfy the hunger created by the aromas from this open-air cookery. Fry bread is also used like a taco, wrapped around a savory filling. But the most delicious fry bread I ever ate was at the Montana home of Michael Dorris and Louise Erdrich. We munched the warm, slightly sweet bread as we drank cool white wine and watched the fading sunlight moving across the valley below.

At my house, I often serve fry bread with one of my soupier chilis so that my guests can use it to sop up the juices. Although the final sprinkling of confectioners' sugar is optional, it is this touch of sweetness that makes this bread truly irresistible. Don't forget that a little bit of sweet will make a very hot chili more palatable.

You can easily double this recipe to make eight breads.

- 2 cups all-purpose flour
- 4 teaspoons baking powder
- 1 teaspoon salt
- 1 teaspoon sugar
- ½ to 1 cup warm water
- Vegetable oil or lard* for frying
- Confectioners' sugar (optional)

1. In a bowl, combine the flour, baking powder, salt, and sugar. Make a hole in the middle of the flour and pour in ½ cup warm water. Mix flour into water with a wooden spoon and add more water as necessary to make a workable dough.
2. Remove the dough to a lightly floured surface and knead for a few minutes, until the dough is smooth and soft. Di-

*Lard is the traditional frying medium, and it is undoubtedly the most delicious. If you can find some fresh lard from a butcher, or are ever inclined to make your own, do make some fry bread fried in lard, so that you know what the real thing is supposed to taste like.

vide the dough into 4 pieces and roll each piece into a ball. Roll out each ball on a lightly floured surface into a ¼-inch-thick round.

3. Heat 2 to 3 inches of oil in an iron frying pan over medium-high heat, until hot but not smoking. Fry one bread at a time, turning it as soon as it becomes golden. Remove when bread is golden brown and puffy. Drain on paper towels or brown paper bags, sprinkle with confectioners' sugar, and serve.

YIELD: *4 breads*

VARIATION:

Indian Tacos

Fry some hamburger meat until it is nicely browned. Drain away the fat and season the meat with salt and pepper. Spread a layer of the meat onto a disk of hot fry bread. Cover the meat with layers of shredded lettuce, shredded cheese, chopped onions, and chopped tomatoes. Finally add a layer of red or green chili sauce. Eat the taco out of hand if you think you can manage, or go ahead and use a knife and fork. Either way, this is delicious Native American food.

> The virile chile—the food that bites back—has branded itself deep into America's palate.
>
> —GUY GARCIA, "Some Like it Hot," *Time* magazine

Over the Chili

Toppings for Chili

The list of toppings for chili is seemingly endless. Traveling around the country, eating in restaurants, road houses, chili parlors, and, best of all, in people's homes, here are some of the toppings I have come across:

- grated cheese: Monterey Jack, cheddar, Gruyère, Parmesan, and Romano
- other cheese: crumbled goat cheese, crumbled feta cheese, and shredded mozzarella
- chopped red or white onions
- chopped scallions
- chopped red or green bell peppers
- chopped tomatoes
- diced avocado
- chopped cilantro
- chopped parsley
- chopped fresh oregano
- chopped olives
- sliced pickled jalapeños
- crushed corn chips
- Tabasco sauce
- vinegar
- lime wedges
- sour cream
- yogurt
- chopped iceberg or romaine lettuce
- chopped roasted peanuts
- toasted pine nuts
- crisp, crumbled bacon

All of these are good, but to my mind the best topping for any chili is one or two of the salsas found on the next few pages. With their vibrant mix of flavors and textures, combining hot, sweet, and tangy tastes, they will transform any chili from a casual dish into a masterpiece. Most take minutes to prepare and can be made several hours ahead. If you take nothing else from this book, I urge you to try some of these salsas with your next bowl of chili.

Now consider this: Slip the burned peel off that mesquite-roasted green chile, chop it together with a ripe tomato, a bit of onion, a minced fresh serrano, and a squeeze of lime juice and you'll then have the ultimate garnish, accompaniment, condiment, and best friend to grilled or smoked food anyone, anywhere, ever stirred up—*salsa!*

—W. PARK KERR, *The El Paso Chile Company's Burning Desires*

Whether you call them salsas (in Spanish) or relishes (in English), these sparkling, chunky mixtures of fruits, herbs, and vegetables are the heart and soul of my cuisine. They are real foods, not just accents. Playing a jazzy counterpoint of piquant and sweet, smooth and crunchy, spicy and cool, they will open your eyes fast . . .

—BOBBY FLAY,
Bobby Flay's Bold American Food

Red Onion Salsa

For this relish the chopped onions are soaked in any icy salt water brine. This removes some bitterness from the onions and accentuates their sweetness. It also gives them a wonderful texture.

- 4 red onions, finely chopped
- 4 tablespoons coarse salt
- 1 cup finely chopped cilantro
- 2 fresh jalapeño chiles, cored, seeded, and finely chopped
- Juice of 1 fresh lime

1. Place the onions in a large bowl and toss together with the salt. Add ice water to just cover. Let stand for 30 minutes.
2. Drain the onion and place in a dry mixing bowl. Add cilantro, jalapeño chiles, and lime juice. Mix well and serve as a topping for chili.

YIELD: *about 2 cups*

VARIATIONS:

1. You can still have a perfectly good relish if you want to skip the salt water soak. Simply combine the chopped onions with the cilantro, jalapeños, and lime juice, add salt to taste, and mix well.
2. Substitute Vidalia onions when they are available, and skip the salt water soak.

Avocado Salsa

When the Spanish arrived they noted with astonishment that the Pueblo Indians were cultivating all manner of beans, squash, melons, wild berries (including strawberries), avocados, and the American plum. The Indians were not great meat eaters but did keep turkeys and prairie hens penned.
—CHRISTOPHER IDONE, *Glorious American Food*

This delicious salsa, which complements just about every chili in this book, is inspired by the recipe in Bobby Flay's brilliant book, *Bold American Food.* If you have any left over, you can serve it as a dip with corn chips, or roll some up in warm tortillas for a great little lunch.

Do look for Hass avocados. They are small, bumpy skinned, with a dense, creamy texture and a wonderful, nutty flavor. When they are ripe, they turn a blackish purple color. Avoid the larger, smooth-skinned, bright green Fuerte avocado, which has watery flesh with little flavor.

- 1 small red onion, finely diced
- 1 small jalapeño, deveined, seeded, and finely diced
- ¼ cup finely chopped cilantro
- 2 tablespoons finely chopped flat-leaf parsley
- ¼ fresh lime juice
- 2 ripe Hass avocados
- Salt and freshly ground black pepper, to taste
- Tabasco sauce, to taste

1. In a medium-size bowl, combine the onion, jalapeño, cilantro, parsley, and lime juice.
2. Cut each avocado in half, remove the pits, peel each half, and chop coarsely into the onion mixture. Toss well, season with salt, pepper, and Tabasco sauce to taste, and serve. You can prepare the salsa up to 1 day ahead, cover with plastic wrap, and refrigerate. Let it come to room temperature before serving.

YIELD: *2 cups*

> **Salsas always put me in a South-of-the-Border mood. Their cool yellows and greens mixed with hot pinks and bright reds make me think of a brilliantly costumed mariachi band. And as for flavors, salsas are like a mini-fiesta for the taste buds: They are at once sharp and sweet, hot and cool.**
>
> —MARK MILLER, *Coyote Cafe*

Pico de Gallo Salsa

Grocery shelves are stocked full with a huge variety of salsas in jars, but not one of them has the fresh, vibrant flavor of this salsa, which you can put together in minutes. Forget fussy procedures like peeling the tomatoes. All you have to do is chop, chop, chop. Avoid the temptation to use your food processor, which will turn your salsa into soup.

You can make Pico de Gallo all year by substituting good-quality canned tomatoes for the fresh, ripe tomatoes of summer.

4 medium-size ripe tomatoes, finely diced
1 small red onion, finely diced
3 jalapeño chiles, cored, seeded, and finely diced
¼ cup finely chopped cilantro
2 teaspoons salt, or more to taste
1 teaspoon sugar
Juice of 1 lime

1. Combine all the ingredients in a bowl and mix well.
2. Serve as a topping for chili, particularly any of the all-bean chilis, or as a dip for tortilla chips.

YIELD: *1½ cups*

Tomatillo Salsa

They may look like small green tomatoes, but tomatillos and tomatoes are not at all related. The tomatillo belongs to the cape gooseberry family, hence its lovely tart flavor. With their affinity for the flavors of green chiles, garlic, and cilantro, tomatillos are an integral part of many salsas and green sauces in southwestern and Mexican cooking.

I like to serve this salsa with any of the red or vegetarian chilis for a refreshing counterpoint.

- 6 medium-size fresh tomatillos, papery husks removed, or 1 can (13 ounces) tomatillos, drained
- 1 small onion, coarsely chopped
- 1 garlic clove
- 1 teaspoon salt
- 1 can (4 ounces) chopped mild green chiles
- 1 fresh jalapeño chile, or 2 fresh serrano chiles, stemmed, seeded, and finely chopped
- ½ cup finely chopped cilantro

1. Place the fresh tomatillos in a small saucepan with enough water to cover. Bring to a boil over high heat, lower the heat a little, and continue cooking the tomatillos for 8 to 10 minutes, until they just start to get tender. Drain. The canned tomatillos do not need to be cooked.
2. Place the tomatillos in a blender or food processor, together with the onion, and blend or process to make a coarse purée. Remove the purée to a serving bowl.
3. With a pestle, crush the garlic clove into the salt in a mortar and mash to a paste. Add ¼ cup water and stir to dissolve. Add this to the puréed tomatillos. Stir in the chopped green chiles, the chopped jalapeño or serrano chiles, and the cilantro. Salt to taste. Let stand at room temperature for 30 minutes before serving. The sauce can be made up to 2 hours ahead, but don't let it stand around too long, for it will lose its bright, fresh taste. If the sauce has thickened, add a little more water and serve.

YIELD: *about 2 cups*

To test salsa, drop some on your tablecloth. If it doesn't burn a hole in your cloth, it is not a good sauce.

—ERNESTINE SEWELL LINCK AND JOYCE GIBSON ROACH, *Eats: A Folk History of Texas Foods*

[Chile] Pepper was so highly valued in ancient Peru that the pods were employed as a medium of exchange. In fact, until the middle of the twentieth century one could purchase things in the plaza of Cuzco with a handful of pepper pods (about 6), known as *rantii*.

—JEAN ANDREWS, *Peppers*

If you have never attended a jalapeño eating contest, a chili cookoff, the Hatch Valley Chile Festival Celebration, the World Green Chile Cookoff or a Louisiana hot pepper eating contest, you haven't lived. On the other hand, perhaps you'd live longer if you didn't. What happened at Woodstock is nothing by comparison. Having never seen a Roman orgy, I can't offer an analogy but I'll wager the only thing different is the substitution of peppers for grapes.

—JEAN ANDREWS, *Peppers*

There is a hot pepper
Pasilla,
One taste and it just
might kill ya,
It's a culinary surprise;
Keep it away from your
eyes.
We're sure you won't try
it . . .
or will ya?

—ANONYMOUS, quoted in *Peppers* by Jean Andrews

Hot Green Chile Salsa

You can vary the heat of this salsa by using different kinds of chiles. Jalapeños will give you a good, moderate heat level. An equal number of serranos will increase the heat level considerably. If you would like to have the salsa hotter still, add a chopped, seeded habanero (only be sure to wear rubber gloves). Habaneros are considered the hottest chiles around, but they also have a wonderful, fruity flavor.

In the Southwest and Mexico, the green chile sauces are always much hotter than any sauces featuring red chiles.

- 2 large ripe tomatoes, finely chopped
- 1 small red onion, finely chopped
- 1 garlic clove, finely minced
- 1 can (4 ounces) chopped hot green chiles, drained
- 1 fresh, mild green chile (Anaheim or California), seeded and finely diced
- 2 to 3 fresh, hot green chiles (serrano or jalapeño), seeded and finely diced
- ½ cup finely chopped cilantro
- 1½ teaspoons salt, or more to taste
- 2 tablespoons fresh lime juice, or more to taste

Combine all the ingredients in a mixing bowl and mix well. Taste and adjust all the seasonings—heat, salt, and tartness to your taste.

YIELD: *about 1½ cups*

Black Bean Salsa

Excellent as a topping for any chili, but especially for any of the all-meat-and-no-beans chilis. Can also be served as a dip with tortilla chips.

- 1½ cups fresh or thawed frozen corn kernels
- 2 cups cooked black beans (see page 92), or 1 can (15 ounces) black beans, drained and rinsed
- 3 medium-size ripe tomatoes, finely diced
- 1 red bell pepper, cored, seeded, and finely diced
- 1 fresh jalapeño or serrano chile, cut into very thin slices
- 1 medium-size red onion, finely diced
- ½ cup finely chopped cilantro
- ⅓ cup best extra-virgin olive oil
- ⅓ cup fresh lime juice
- 1 teaspoon salt
- ¼ teaspoon cayenne, or to taste

1. Drop the corn kernels into boiling water, reduce heat to low, and cook for 3 minutes. Rinse under cold running water to stop the cooking, and drain.
2. Combine the corn kernels, black beans, tomatoes, red bell pepper, jalapeño or serrano chile, onion, and cilantro in a large bowl and mix well.
3. In a small bowl, combine the olive oil, lime juice, salt, and cayenne and whisk together.
4. Pour the olive oil mixture over the beans and mix well. Let stand for at least 1 hour before serving so the flavors can blend. Or, you can make this 1 day ahead and keep it covered in the refrigerator. Let the salsa come to room temperature before serving.

YIELD: *about 4 cups*

The most important thing to remember about salsas is that, like the Latin dance that shares their name, the best ones are wild, loose, and loud. . . . I suggest you take the same loose and easy attitude toward the way you serve these salsas. You can serve them with any entrée from grilled fish to roast meats to stews. Use them to add lively, healthful flavor to steamed vegetables, or to brighten up heavier starch dishes like rice or beans. Of course, you can always just scoop them up with tortilla chips or deep-fried plantains or whatever is the scooping utensil of your choice. The point is, there are no rules here, so just suit yourself. You really can't go wrong.

—CHRIS SCHLESINGER AND JOHN WILLOUGHBY, *Salsas, Sambals, Chutneys & Chowchows*

Under the Chili

> Wish I had time for just one more bowl of chili.
>
> —ALLEGED DYING WORDS OF KIT CARSON,
> quoted in *A Bowl of Red*

Under the Chili, or What to Serve the Chili On

Many of the chilis in this book don't require a foundation of starch, and this is especially true of the meat chilis in the front of the book. However, the soupier chilis, the chilis with beans, the green chilis, and the vegetarian chilis, are often happier sitting on a scoop of rice, a bed of spaghetti, nestled into a baked squash, or even plopped over some roast potatoes. These not only add texture and flavor, often rounding out a very spicy chili, but also stretch the amount of chili you have to serve more people.

Here, then, is a selection of underpinnings for any chili that you make.

Basic Buttered Rice

In my experience, even people who claim to disdain rice with their chili tend to help themselves quite liberally when a pot of steaming rice is placed on the chili buffet table. In fact, any number of times when planning a chili party, I have cooked such huge quantities of rice that I was sure I'd be living on the leftovers for the rest of the year. But to my surprise, and sometimes dismay, the rice would often disappear long before the chili and I would end up rushing to the stove to put on more.

Planting rice is never fun;
Bent from morn till set of sun;
Cannot stand and cannot sit;
Cannot rest for a little bit.

—FROM AN OLD FILIPINO SONG, quoted in *The Staffs of Life*, by E. J. Kahn, Jr.

- 1½ cups long-grain rice
- 3 cups water
- 2 tablespoons unsalted butter
- 1 teaspoon salt

1. Place the rice in a saucepan together with the water, butter, and salt. Bring to a boil, stir, and reduce heat to very low. Cover the saucepan and cook for 15 to 20 minutes, until the rice has absorbed all the water.
2. Let stand, covered, for 5 to 10 minutes before serving.

YIELD: *6 servings*

NOTE: Any leftover rice can be refrigerated for several days or frozen in airtight containers for several months. Reheat in a double boiler or microwave.

In many ancient languages, "rice" is synonymous with "food." *Dhanya,* the Indian word for rice, means "sustainer of the human race." (The name of the sixth-century-B.C. king of Nepal, Suddhodana, who was the father of the Gautama Buddha, means "Pure Rice.") A thousand years before Christ, Japan was called "Mizumono Kuni"—"The Land of Luxuriant Rice Crops."

—E. J. KAHN, JR., *The Staffs of Life*

Green Rice

This is a lovely herb-scented rice with a subtle tang of lemon. Its fresh, green flavors make good companions to any of the red chilis. The recipe may be cut in half, or any leftovers may be frozen for up to 6 weeks.

- 2 tablespoons butter or olive oil
- 1 small onion, finely chopped
- 2 cups long-grain rice
- 4 cups boiling water
- ½ teaspoon salt
- ¼ cup finely chopped cilantro
- ¼ cup finely chopped parsley
- 6 scallions, thinly sliced
- Juice of ½ lemon

1. Heat the butter or olive oil in a medium-size saucepan over high heat. Add the onion and cook, stirring, for 2 minutes. Add the rice, lower heat to medium, and cook, stirring, for about 3 minutes, until every grain of rice is coated with butter or oil.
3. Pour in the boiling water and salt. Stir once, lower the heat to very low, and simmer, tightly covered, for about 20 minutes, until all the liquid is absorbed.
4. Remove from heat, add the cilantro, parsley, scallions, and lemon juice. Toss with a fork to mix well, and serve.

YIELD: *8 servings*

Green Chile Rice Casserole

This is a rich and delectable dish. It reminds me of a rice pudding, only with spicy, savory flavors. It makes a very attractive presentation on a buffet table and happily accompanies any of the chilis in the book. But it makes an especially pleasing partner to any of the vegetarian chilis.

The recipe can easily be cut in half to serve a smaller number of people.

- 2 cups long-grain rice
- ½ teaspoon salt
- 3 tablespoons unsalted butter
- 2 cups sour cream, or reduced-fat sour cream
- ¼ to ½ teaspoon cayenne, or to taste
- 2 cups grated Monterey Jack cheese
- 2 cans (4 ounces each) chopped mild green chiles
- ¼ cup freshly grated Parmesan cheese

1. Bring 4 cups of water to a boil in a medium-size saucepan. Add the rice, salt, and 2 tablespoons of the butter. Stir well, reduce heat to low, cover the pan, and simmer for 20 minutes, until the liquid is absorbed. Remove from the heat and uncover the rice to let it cool.
2. Preheat the oven to 350° F.
3. Grease the bottom and sides of a medium-size casserole. Mix the cooled rice with the sour cream and cayenne and spread half the rice mixture on the bottom. Sprinkle the grated Monterey Jack cheese over the rice and arrange the chiles on top. Cover with the remaining rice, sprinkle with Parmesan, and dot with remaining butter.
4. Bake for 30 minutes, until the top turns golden and crusty.

YIELD: *8 to 10 servings*

The French have never found out how to cook rice.

—ELIZABETH DAVID, *Italian Food*

Capsicums [chiles] are not only good, they are good for you. Nutritionally, capsicums are a dietary plus. They contain more vitamin A than any other food plant and are also an excellent source of vitamin C and the B vitamins. By gram weight, jalapeños contain at least twenty times more vitamin A and more than twice the vitamin C than fresh oranges. Capsicums also contain significant amounts of magnesium, iron, thiamine, riboflavin, and niacin.

—JEAN ANDREWS, *Red Hot Peppers*

Brown Rice Pilaf

> Once upon a time, the Malaysians say, rice had to be harvested from the fields: it is man's own fault that he now has to eat rice, as he eats bread, by the sweat of his brow. Every day, the story goes, a single rice grain would appear in the farmer's house and make its way into the cooking pot. The housewife knew that she had to cook the grain without ever opening the lid; if she kept the taboo intact the pot would be ready by the afternoon, full of cooked rice. But one of her children ignored her warnings one day, and peeked into the pot. It is said that what the child saw was a small girl crouching inside—and the damage was done. The girl was angry at having been seen, and from that day onward, rice for man has meant backbreaking labour.
>
> —MARGARET VISSER, *Much Depends on Dinner*

I like the chewy, moist texture of short-grain brown rice, but the long-grain brown rice will work just as well in this recipe. If you find that you don't have time for the preliminary soaking, simply add an extra cup of water to the rice and 15 minutes additional cooking time.

- 2 cups short-grain brown rice
- 2 tablespoons olive oil
- 1 large onion, finely chopped
- 3 cups boiling water
- 1 teaspoon salt, or to taste

1. Wash the brown rice in several changes of cold water and soak it in cold water for 1 hour.
2. Place olive oil and onion in a large heavy pot and sauté over medium heat for 5 minutes.
3. Drain the rice and add it to the onions. Cook, stirring, over medium heat until rice is coated with oil and is starting to brown slightly, 10 to 15 minutes.
4. Add the water and salt, turn the heat to low, stir well, cover, and cook over low heat for 30 minutes, or until the water has been absorbed and the rice is tender but slightly *al dente.* Turn off the heat and let stand in covered pot for 10 to 15 minutes before serving.

YIELD: *7 cups cooked rice*

NOTE: Whenever I cook brown rice I always try to make extra, because it is so useful to have on hand. I add it to soup, turn it into a quick salad, support a stir-fry, even cook it with some milk and raisins for a breakfast cereal.

Cooked rice can be refrigerated in a plastic container for a week, or frozen for as long as six weeks. It reheats perfectly in a microwave oven, or in a nonstick pan with a few tablespoons of water.

Millet

A nice alternative to rice, millet is a wonderful companion to strongly flavored foods like chili.

- 1 tablespoon olive oil or butter
- 1 cup millet
- 2 cups boiling water
- ½ teaspoon salt

1. Rinse the millet in several changes of cold water and drain.
2. In a heavy 2-quart saucepan, heat the oil or butter over medium-high heat together with the millet. Cook, stirring with a wooden spoon, to dry out and toast the millet. Continue cooking and stirring until the millet develops a nice toasted aroma like popcorn, 5 to 10 minutes.
3. Turn off the heat and pour in the hot water. Stand back a little to avoid sputtering. Stir in the salt and, over medium heat, bring the water to a boil. Reduce the heat to low, cover the pot, and simmer for 20 to 25 minutes, until all the liquid has been absorbed. Turn off the heat and let stand, covered, for another 5 minutes.
4. Fluff millet with a fork and serve.

YIELD: *4 cups*

Millet is one of the most nutritious of the grain family, easy to digest, rich in essential amino acids, phosphorous, and B vitamins, with an iron content higher than any grain except amaranth.

—SHERYL AND MEL LONDON, *Creative Cooking With Grains and Pasta*

Millet stands up to strong flavors and is a good grain to serve with assertively flavored entrées.

—LORNA J. SASS, *Recipes from an Ecological Kitchen*

Byron had a beautiful Venetian mistress who used to float with him in a gondola down the Grand Canal, lazily nibbling bits of polenta from a ball of it which she kept warm down the front of her dress, between her breasts.

—MARGARET VISSER, *Much Depends on Dinner*

Polenta

Polenta is most certainly associated with Italy, but it is not much different from the all-American cornmeal mush. Not surprisingly, the hearty corn flavor and soft soothing texture of polenta make it a terrific companion to almost any chili. It is especially good with the bean-filled vegetarian chilis.

The most basic polenta is nothing but water, salt, and cornmeal. If you want to make that, simply omit the other ingredients. But the addition of butter and garlic to the cooking water transforms an ordinary dish of mush into something quite tasty and extraordinary. As for the method of making polenta, there are various approaches. Some cooks like to make a paste with the cornmeal and cold water before stirring it into the hot water; some insist on the classic method of stirring a fine stream of cornmeal into violently boiling water. The method described below is easy and lump-free, and you don't have to stand over boiling water.

7 cups water
1 teaspoon salt
3 tablespoons unsalted butter
3 garlic cloves, crushed
2 cups coarsely ground cornmeal

1. Bring the water to a boil in a large heavy pot. (The water should not come more than halfway up the sides of the pot.) Turn off the heat. Stir in salt, butter, and garlic. Then stir in cornmeal, pouring it in a fine, steady stream as you stir.
2. Place the pot over medium-high heat and continue stirring as the cornmeal boils and thickens. Make sure to use a long-handled wooden spoon and to stand back from the pot so the bubbles don't explode in your face. As the cornmeal thickens, the boiling mass might get violent. Simply turn off the heat and keep stirring. When it has calmed down, turn up the heat and continue cooking until done. The total cooking time is usually 15 to 20 minutes. The polenta is done when it forms a very thick mass and starts to

pull away from the sides of the pot as you stir. Serve hot as a base for any chili that has lots of gravy.

YIELD: *6 to 8 servings*

VARIATIONS: Fried or grilled polenta is good when you want to make part of the meal ahead. It is also a good way to serve polenta to a large crowd.

Fried Polenta: Make polenta as described above, then pour into an oiled 9 × 5 × 3-inch loaf pan or 9 × 12-inch roasting pan and cover with plastic wrap. Refrigerate for several hours or overnight. (The dimensions of both the loaf pan and the roasting pan are not critical; use any pans you have that are about that size.) Cut polenta into ½-inch slices or into squares, triangles, or even circles, using a cookie cutter. Heat about 2 tablespoons olive oil or olive oil mixed with butter in a large skillet and fry the polenta pieces until golden brown on both sides.

Grilled Polenta: Prepare polenta as for fried polenta. Brush polenta pieces with olive oil on each side and grill over hot coals or under a broiler for about 2 minutes on each side, until golden brown.

Fried mush came along in the fall, after the first harvest of winter corn and before the pancake season set in, and again in the spring when the batter pitcher was washed and put away. Fried mush for breakfast followed a preceding supper of mush and milk. My mother made her mush by sifting yellow corn meal, fresh from the mill, into an iron kettle of boiling salted water; with one hand she sifted the meal while with the other she stirred it with a wooden spoon. It was then drawn to the back of the stove to bubble and sputter and spurt for an hour or longer—and woe to you if it happened to spurt onto bare hand or arm while stirring.

What ever mush was left over after supper was packed into a greased bread tin. In the morning this was sliced and fried in hot fat, and eaten with butter and syrup.

—DELLA T. LUTES,
The Country Kitchen

Corn, beans, and squash were always eaten together and always planted together: In Iroquois myth they were represented as three inseparable sisters. When the plants emerged from the hill, the corn grew straight and strong, the beans climbed the corn, and the squash plant trailed down the side of the hill and covered the flat land between the mounds.

—MARGARET VISSER, *Much Depends on Dinner*

Roasted Acorn Squash

The quantity in this recipe depends on how many people you are serving. Select one acorn squash for every two people. I always like to make a few extra, for people who want seconds, or for leftovers the next day.

Acorn squash, 1 for every 2 people
Melted butter
Salt
Brown sugar
Orange juice

1. Preheat the oven to 400° F.
2. Cut acorn squash in half, either across the midsection or lengthwise. Scoop out the seeds and stringy parts. Brush the cut surfaces with melted butter and sprinkle with salt.
3. Arrange the squash in a baking pan, cut side down, and film the bottom of the pan with ¼ inch of water. Bake for 30 minutes.
4. Turn the squash over, brush insides with melted butter, and sprinkle with brown sugar. Bake for 15 to 30 minutes longer, until tender, basting occasionally with a tablespoon or two of orange juice.

Mail-Order Sources

Elizabeth Berry
Gallina Canyon Ranch
144 Camino Escondido
Santa Fe, New Mexico 87501
tel: (505) 982-4194
fax: (505) 986-0936

Elizabeth Berry grows unusual varieties of chiles and beans. So if you'd like to try some Black Ying Yang beans or Christmas Lima beans, or to sample a Dried Apple Chile, here is the place to shop. I like to call and ask Ms. Berry to put a selection together for me of the best of whatever she's got at the moment. One of my absolute favorite places to shop.

Los Chileros de Nueva Mexico
P.O. Box 6215
Santa Fe, New Mexico 87502
tel: (505) 471-6967

Whole dried chiles, chile powders, fresh and frozen green chiles in season, chicos, and other southwestern ingredients.

The Chile Shop
109 East Water Street
Santa Fe, New Mexico 87501
tel: (505) 983-6080

Whole dried chiles, chile powders, and other southwestern ingredients.

Dean & Deluca
560 Broadway
New York, New York 10012
tel: (800) 221-7714 or (212) 431-1691

Dried chiles, chile powders, canned chiles, and a very good selection of current crop beans.

Preferred Meats
P.O. Box 565854
Dallas, Texas 75207
tel: (214) 421-7191

Venison and other game, meats, and poultry.

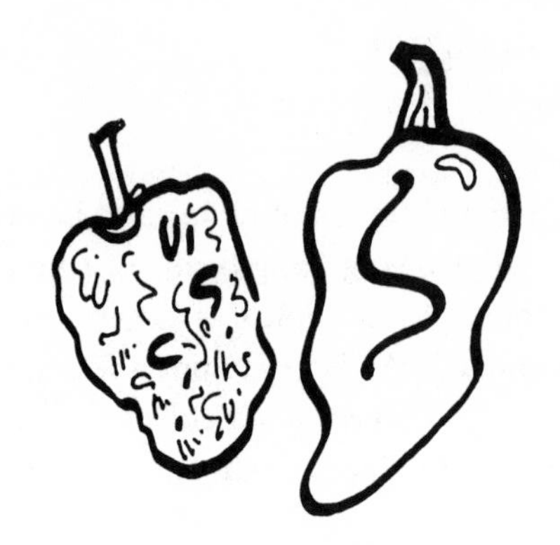

Bibliography: Works Cited and Consulted in the Text

BOOKS

Adams, Ramon F. *Come an' Get It: The Story of the Old Cowboy Cook.* Norman, OK: University of Oklahoma Press, 1952.

Andrews, Jean. *Peppers.* Austin: University of Texas Press, 1984.

———*Red Hot Peppers.* New York: Macmillan Publishing Company, 1993.

Beard, Henry, and Roy McKie. *Cooking: A Dictionary.* New York: Workman Publishing Co., 1985.

Benét, Stephen Vincent. *Selected Works of Stephen Vincent Benét, Volume 1.* New York: Henry Holt & Company, 1963.

Bennett, Victor. *The Complete Bean Cookbook.* Englewood Cliffs, NJ: Prentice-Hall, 1967.

Bridges, Bill. *The Great Chili Book.* Berkeley, CA: Ten Speed Press, 1991.

Brown, Ellen. *Southwest Tastes.* New York: HP Books, 1987.

Butel, Jane. *Chili Madness.* New York: Workman Publishing Co., 1980.

Carruth, Gorton, and Eugene Ehrlich. *The Harper Book of American Quotations.* New York: Harper & Row, 1988.

Cooper, Joe. *With or Without Beans.* Dallas, TX: William S. Henson, 1952.

David, Elizabeth. *Italian Food.* Harmondsworth, Middlesex, England: Penguin, 1973.

Dent, Huntley. *The Feast of Santa Fe.* New York: Simon & Schuster, 1985.

DeWitt, David, and Mary Jane Wilan. *The Food Lover's Handbook to the Southwest.* Rocklin, CA: Prima Publishing, 1992.

——— and Melissa T. Stock. *Hot and Spicy and Meatless.* Rocklin, CA: Prima Publishing, 1994.

——— and Nancy Gerlach. *The Whole Chile Pepper Book.* Boston: Little, Brown & Co., 1985.

Dobie, J. Frank. *A Taste of Texas.* Dallas, TX: Nieman-Marcus, 1949.

Donadio, Stephen, et al. *The New York Public Library Book of 20th Century American Quotations.* New York: Warner Books, 1992.

DuSablon, Mary Anna. *Cincinnati Recipe Treasury.* Athens, OH: Ohio University Press, 1983.

Fischer, Al, and Mildred Fischer. *Chili Lovers' Cook Book:* Phoenix, AZ: Golden West Publishers, 1984.

Flay, Bobby. *Bobby Flay's Bold American Food.* New York: Warner Books, 1994.

Griffith, Dotty. *Wild About Chili.* Hauppage, NY: Barron's, 1985.

Hardeman, Nicholas. *Shucks, Shocks, and Hominy Blocks.* Baton Rouge, LA: Louisiana State University Press, 1981.

Hazen-Hammond, Susan. *Chile Pepper Fever.* Stillwater, MN: Voyageur Press, Inc., 1993.

Hughes, Stella. *Bacon & Beans: Ranch-Country Recipes.* Colorado Springs: The Western Horseman Inc., 1990.

Idone, Christopher, and Tom Eckerle. *Glorious American Food.* New York: Stewart, Tabori & Chang, 1985.

Jamison, Cheryl Alters, and Bill Jamison. *The Rancho de Chimayó Cookbook.* Boston: The Harvard Common Press, 1991.

Kahn, E. J. *The Staffs of Life.* New York: Little, Brown & Co., 1985.

Keegan, Marcia. *Southwest Indian Cookbook.* Weehawken, NJ: Clear Light Publications, 1987.

Kerr, W. Park, and Michael McLaughlin. *The El Paso Chile Company's Burning Desires.* New York: William Morrow and Company, Inc., 1994.

Kolpas, Norman. *The Chili Cookbook.* Los Angeles: Price Stern Sloan, 1991.

Laden, Alice, and R. J. Minney. *The George Bernard Shaw Vegetarian Cookbook.* New York: Pyramid, 1974.

Lawrence, D. H. *Sea and Sardinia.* London: Heinemann, 1968.

Linck, Ernestine Sewell, and Joyce Gibson Roach. *Eats: A Folk History of Texas Foods.* Fort Worth: Texas Christian University Press, 1989.

London, Sheryl and Mel London. *Creative Cooking with Grains and Pasta.* Emmans, PA: Rodale Press, 1982.

Lutes, Della T. *The Country Kitchen.* Boston: Little, Brown & Co., 1937.

Metcalf, Fred, ed. *The Penguin Dictionary of Modern Humorous Quotations.* London: Penguin Books, 1987.

Miller, Mark. *Coyote Cafe.* Berkeley, CA: Ten Speed Press, 1989.

———*The Great Chile Book.* Berkeley, CA: Ten Speed Press, 1991.

Naj, Amal. *Peppers: A Story of Hot Pursuits.* New York: Alfred A. Knopf, 1992.

Neely, William and Martina Neely. *The International Chili Society's Official Chili Cookbook.* New York: St. Martin's Press, 1981.

Pyles, Stephen, and John Harisson. *The New Texas Cuisine.* Garden City, NY: Doubleday & Company, 1993.

Robbins, Maria Polushkin. *A Cook's Alphabet of Quotations.* New York: Dutton, 1991.

Rozin, Elisabeth. *Blue Corn and Chocolate.* New York: Alfred A. Knopf, 1992.

Sass, Lorna. *Recipes from an Ecological Kitchen.* New York: William Morrow and Company, Inc., 1992.

Schlesinger, Chris, and John Willoughby. *Salsas, Sambals, Chutneys & Chowchows.* New York: William Morrow and Company, Inc., 1993.

Shannon, Bette. *Green Chili.* Tucson, AZ: Treasure Chest Publications, 1981.

Society for Range Management. *Trail Boss's Cowboy Cookbook.* Helena, MT: Falcon Press, 1985.

Sokolov, Raymond. *Fading Feast.* New York: Farrar, Straus & Giroux, 1981.

———*Why We Eat What We Eat.* New York: Summit Books, 1991.

Steinbeck, John. *Tortilla Flat.* New York: Viking Penguin, 1977.

Stevenson, Burton. *The Home Book of Quotations, Tenth Edition.* New York: Dodd Mead & Company, 1967.

Sweet, Alexander. *Alex Sweet's Texas.* Austin, TX: University of Texas Press, 1986.

Tannahill, Reay. *Food in History.* New York: Stein and Day Publishers, 1973.

Tolbert, Frank X. *A Bowl of Red.* Garden City, NY: Doubleday & Company, 1972.

Trillin, Calvin. *American Fried: Adventures of a Happy Eater.* Garden City, NY: Doubleday & Company, 1974.

Trollope, Frances. *Domestic Manners of the Americans.* London: Century Publishing Co., Ltd., 1984.

Visser, Margaret. *Much Depends on Dinner.* New York: Macmillan, 1988.

Whittier, John Greenleaf. "The Corn Song," in the poem "The Huskers." *Songs of Labor,* 1850

MAGAZINES AND NEWSPAPERS

Garcia, Guy, "Some Like it Hot," *Time,* October 12, 1992.

King, Wayne, "Champion Chili," *Food & Wine,* March, 1994.

Smith, H. Allen, "Nobody Knows More About Chili Than I Do," *Travel/Holiday,* August, 1967.

Stock, Melissa T., "Viva Terlingua," *Chile Pepper,* October, 1993.

———"Talking Pods: Tony Hillerman," *Chile Pepper,* October, 1993.

Index

Acorn squash, roasted, 124
Adams, Ramon F., 9, 50, 86, 104
American Fried (Trillin), 33, 78
Anaheim chiles, 44–45
Anasazi beans, 83
Ancho chiles, 2
Andrews, Jean, 6, 76, 113, 114, 119
Andy Weil's Vegetarian Chili, 64–65
Avocado
  about, ix
  Salsa, 111

Bacon & Beans, Ranch-Country Recipes (Hughes), 5, 90, 93
Baldwin, Mark, 32
Basic
  Buttered Rice, 117
  Skillet Corn Bread, 96
Bean and Corn Chili, 68–69
Beans
  about, 83–84
  black bean recipes, 18–19, 22–23, 29, 66–67, 92, 115
  Chili Beans, 87
  cooking tips, 84–85
  Cowboy Beans, 86
  Drunken Pinto Beans, 90–91
  Refried Beans, 93
  Stewed Pinto Beans, 88–89
Beard, Henry, 34
Beef
  pork green chili with, 50–51
  Sirloin Chili with Black Beans, 29
  See also Chile con carne
Benét, Stephen Vincent, 97
Berger, Shelley, 24
Black beans, 83
  confetti chili with, 66–67
  lamb chili with, 22–23
  recipe for, 92
  salsa, 115
  sirloin chili with, 29
  venison chili with, 18–19
Blue Corn and Chocolate (Rozin), 26, 56, 69, 96
Bold American Food (Flay), 98, 110, 111
Boldenweck, Bill, 62
Bowl of Red, A (Tolbert), vii, 3, 7, 11, 12, 19, 24, 35, 51, 116
Breads, 94–95
  Basic Skillet Corn Bread, 96
  Chile Carrot Corn Bread, 100
  Corn Sticks, 101
  Easy Corn Muffins, 97
  Green Chile Corn Bread, 98–99
  Navajo Fry Bread, 106–107
  Piñon Corn Bread, 102–103
  Sourdough Biscuits, 104–105
Brent's Chicken Chili for a Party, 20–21
Bresnick, Paul, 30
Bridges, Bill, vii, 18, 37, 40, 60, 82
Brown Rice Pilaf, 120
Butel, Jane, 20

Capsaicin
  about, 60
  caution for, 2, 44
Carne Adobada, vii, 13
Carson, Kit, 116
Chicken
  Chili in Beer, 24–25
  Chili for a Party, 20–21
  Chili Verde, 58–59
  green chiles with, 60
Chicos, 68–69
Chile
  Carrot Corn Bread, 100
  chipotle, ix
  con Tempeh, 76–77
  green 44–46
  machismo and, 26
  nutrition of, 119
  red, 2–4
Chile Pepper Fever (Hazen-Hammond), 38, 48, 70, 72
Chile Pepper magazine, 16, 47
Chili
  Beans, 87
  Blanco, 58–59
  con carne, 12, 15, 40–41, 48–49
  -mac, 37
  origins of, 8
  Parlor Chili, 34–35
  powder, 4, 5
  toppings for, 108–109

Chili Lovers' Cook Book (Fischer), 47
Chili Madness (Butel), 20
Chiltecpin chiles, 3, 6
Chimayó Chile Powder, 3
Chipps, Genie, 26
Christmas Picadillo, 38–39
Chuck Wagon Chili, 8–9
Cilantro, ix
Cincinnati chilis
  4-way turkey, 36–37
  Gary's, 32–33
Columbus, Christopher, 52
Come an' Get It: The Story of the Old Cowboy Cook (Adams), 9, 50, 84, 86, 104
Complete Bean Cookbook, The, 85
Cooking beans, 84–85
Cooking: A Dictionary (Beard & McKie), 34
Corn
  and Bean Chili, 68–69
  Polenta, 122–123
Corn breads, 94–95
  Basic Skillet Corn Bread, 96
  Chile Carrot Corn Bread, 100
  Corn Sticks, 101
  Easy Corn Muffins, 97
  Green Chile Corn Bread, 98–99
  Piñon Corn Bread, 102–103
Cousins, Margaret, 11, 35
Cowboy
  Beans, 86
  Chuck Wagon Chili, 8–9
Coyote Cafe (Miller), 112
Cumin *(comino)*, ix–x

David, Elizabeth, 119
Dent, Huntley, 106
Derby Day Chili, 26–28
Dewitt, David, 17, 92
Dirkson, Senator Everett, 85
Disease, chiles and, 72
Dobie, J. Frank, 79
Domenici, Senator Pete, 4
Dorris, Michael, 106
Drug Store Chili, 35
Drunken Pinto Beans, 90–91

East Coast Chili Con Carne, 40–41
Easy Corn Muffins, 97
Eats: A Folk History of Texas Foods (Linck & Roach), 88, 113
El Paso Chile Company's Burning Desires, The (Kerr), 109
Epazote, x
Erdrich, Louise, 106

Fading Feast (Sokolov), 22
Feast of Santa Fe, The (Dent), 106
Fischer, Al and Mildred, 47
Fisher, M. F. K., 94
Flay, Bobby, 98, 110
Food Lover's Handbook to the Southwest, The, vii, 17, 92
Fried Polenta, 123
Fry bread, 106–107

Garcia, Guy, 108
Gary's Cincy Chili, 32–33
Gebhardt's Chili Powder, 34
Great Chili Book, The (Bridges), vii, 18, 37, 40, 60, 64, 82
Green chile
  about, 44–45
  Corn Bread, 98–99
  Hot Salsa, 114
  Rice Casserole, 119
  roasting and peeling, 45–46
  Stew, 47
  with Chicken, 60
Green chilis
  Beef and Pork Green Chili, 50–51
  Chicken Chili Verde, 58–59
  Green Chiles with Chicken, 60
  Green Chile Stew, 57
  Green Chili Con Carne, 48–49
  Navajo Green Chili with Lamb, 52–53
  Shrimps in Green Chile Sauce, 54–55
  Turkey Albondigas in Green Chile Sauce, 56–57
Green Rice, 118
Grilled Polenta, 123

Hazen-Hammond, Susan, 38, 48, 70, 72
Hillerman, Tony, 47
Homemade Chili Powder Blend, 5
Hot Green Chile Salsa, 114
Hughes, Stella, 5, 90, 93

Idone, Christopher, 103, 111
Illness, chiles and, 72
Indian Tacos, 107
Ingredients, ix–x
International Chili Society's Official Chili Cookbook (Neely), viii, 8, 27, 54

Jalapeño chiles, 44
James, Harry, 24
Jamison, Cheryl Alters and Bill, 4, 58
Johnson, Mrs. Lyndon B., 17, 19

Kahn, E. J., Jr., 117, 118
Kerr, W. Park, 109
Kidney beans, 83
King, Wayne, 30
Kiradjieff, Tom, 32

Lady Bird Johnson's Pedernales River Chile, 17
Lamb
  Chili with Black Beans, 22–23
  Navajo green chili with, 52–53
Lawrence, D. H., 63
Linck, Ernestine Sewell, 88, 113
London, Sheryl and Mel, 121
Lutes, Della T., 123

Machismo, chiles and, 26
Mail-order sources, 125–126
Manly, William Lewis, 48
Many Vegetable Vegetarian Chili, 78–79
Maria's Big Party Chili, 14–16
McKie, Roy, 34
Meat
  choosing, viii
  cutting, 7
Meatballs, turkey in green chile sauce, 56–57
Miller, Mark, 64, 112
Millet, 121
Moore, Gordon, 24
Morton, J. B., 67
Muffins and corn breads, 94–95
  Easy Corn Muffins, 97

Naj, Amal, 74
Navajo
  Fry Bread, 106–107
  Green Chili with Lamb, 52–53
Neely, Martina and William, 8, 54
New Mexican Red Chile Pork, 12–13
New Mexico
  green chiles, 44–45
  red chiles, 3
Newsom, Brent, 20
New Texas Cuisine, The (Pyles), 29
No-Nonsense Bowl of Red, 6–7
Nutrition, chiles and, 119

Olive oil, x
Oregano, x

Pasilla chiles, 3
Pedernales River recipe, 7, 17
Peeling green chiles, 45–46
Peppers (Andrews), 6, 76, 113, 114, 119
Peppers: A Story of Hot Pursuits (Naj), 74
Picadillo, 38–39
Pico de Gallo Salsa, 112
Pilaf, brown rice, 120
Piñon Corn Bread, 102–103
Pinto beans, 83
  chili-style, 87
  cowboy-style, 86
  drunken-style, 90–91
  stewed, 88–89
Piquine chiles, 3
Poblano chiles, 2
Polenta, 122
Pork
  and beef green chili, 50–51
  New Mexican red chile, 12–13
Pyles, Stephen, 29

Rancho de Chimayó Cookbook, The (Jamison), 4, 58
Red chiles, about, 2–4
Red chilis
  Brent's Chicken Chili for a Party, 20–21
  Chicken Chili in Beer, 24–25
  Christmas Picadillo, 38–39
  Cincinnati 4-Way Turkey Chili, 36–37
  Cowboy Chuck Wagon Chili, 8–9
  Derby Day Chili, 26–28
  East Coast Chili Con Carne, 40–41
  Gary's Cincy Chili, 32–33
  Homemade Chili Powder Blend, 5
  Lady Bird Johnson's Pedernales River Chile, 17

Red chilis (Cont.)
  Lamb Chili with Black Beans, 22–23
  Maria's Big Party Chili, 14–16
  Midwest Chili Parlor Chili, 34–35
  New Mexican Red Chile Pork, 12–13
  No-Nonsense Bowl of Red, 6–7
  Sirloin Chili with Black Beans, 29
  Southern Seafood Chili, 30–31
  Tofu in Red Chile Sauce, 74–75
  Venison Chili with Black Beans, 18–19
  Winter Solstice Chili, 10–11
Red Onion Salsa, 110
Redd, Annaley, 89
Refried Beans, 93
Rice
  basic buttered, 117
  brown rice pilaf, 120
  casserole with green chiles, 119
  green, 118
Rieveschl, Gary, 32
Roach, Joyce Gibson, 88, 113
Roasted Acorn Squash, 124
Roasting green chiles, 45–46
Rogers, Will, vii
Rosenzweig, Anne, 10
Rozin, Elizabeth, 26, 56, 69, 96

Sag Harbor's Vegetarian Chili, 72–73
Salsa
  avocado, 111
  black bean, 115
  hot green chile, 114
  Pico de Gallo, 112
  red onion, 110
  tomatillo, 113
Salsas, Sambals, Chutneys & Chowchows (Schlesinger & Willoughby), 115
Sass, Lorna J., 121
Schlesinger, Chris, 115
Schliepake, Willie, 51
Seafood chili, 30–31
Serrano chiles, 45
Shaw, George Bernard, 66
Shelby, Carroll, 27
Shrimps in Green Chile Sauce, 54–55
Sirloin Chili with Black Beans, 29
Smith, H. Allen, viii, 34, 73
Sokolov, Raymond, 22, 52
Sourdough Biscuits, 104–105
Southern Seafood Chili, 30–31
Spaghetti, chili-mac, 37
Staffs of Life, The (Kahn), 117, 118
Standish, Miles, IV, 2
Steinbeck, John, 84, 87
Stewed Pinto Beans, 88–89
Stock, Melissa T., 16
Sweet, Alexander, 15

Taste of Texas, A (Dobie), 79
Taylor, Tex, 84, 104
Tempeh, chili con, 76–77
Tepin chiles, 3
Texas-style chili, 7
Tofu in Red Chile Sauce, 74–75
Tolbert, Frank X., vii, 3, 7, 11, 12, 19, 24, 35, 51
Tomatillo Salsa, 113
Toppings for chili, 108–109
Trail Boss's Cowboy Cookbook, 8, 10, 89
Trillin, Calvin, 33, 78
Trollope, Frances, 100
Turkey
  Albondigas in Green Chile Sauce, 56–57
  chili, Cincinnati-style, 36–37
TVP (textured vegetable protein), 73

Vegetable Broth, 62–63
Vegetarian chilis
  Andy Weil's Vegetarian Chili, 64–65
  Bean and Corn Chili, 68–69
  Black Bean Confetti Chili, 66–67
  Chile con Tempeh, 76–77
  Many Vegetable Vegetarian Chili, 78–79
  Sag Harbor's Vegetarian Chili, 72–73
  Tofu in Red Chile Sauce, 74–75
  Vegetarian White Bean Chili, 70–71
Venison Chili with Black Beans, 18–19
Visser, Margaret, 101, 102, 120, 122, 124

Weil, Dr. Andrew, 64
White bean chili, vegetarian, 70–71
White beans, 83
White Chili, 58–59
Whole Chile Pepper Book, The (Standish), 2
Why We Eat What We Eat (Sokolov), 52
Wilan, Mary Jane, 17, 92
Willoughby, John, 115
Winter Solstice Chili, 10–11
With or Without Beans (Cooper), viii